Endor$

Jenifer Jernigan is a fresh new voice to the world of Bible study. If you're looking to *Dive Deeper*, you'll love this study! One thing is certain: Jenifer delivers what she promises. From the start, I was drawn right in. Not only did I enjoy Jenifer's study, I enjoyed *her*!

—Tammie Head
Bible Teacher and Author of *Duty or Delight*

In a world where many are hungry for God's truth, Bible studies that don't just spoon feed are desperately needed. I so very much appreciate Jenifer's approach to Bible study in *Dive Deeper: Finding Deep Faith Beyond Shallow Religion*. *Dive Deeper* is both challenging and encouraging as Jenifer leads the reader to not only glean from the book of Ephesians but gain confidence to study the Bible for themselves. With a relatable and vulnerable voice, readers will fall in love with Jenifer Jernigan and see her as a teacher and friend.

—Sarah Francis Martin
InScribed Studies author of *Just RISE UP!: A Call To Make Jesus Famous*
www.liveitoutblog.com

As one who has spent countless hours strolling along the seashore searching for tiny treasures, I understand the need for diving deeper to discover those hidden treasures revealed to us by God when we dive deeper. I so appreciate Jenifer's deep yet simplistic technique for helping us take the plunge into Ephesians. Her delightful personality comes to the forefront through her humor and honesty making it such a fun swim.

—Margaret N. Kennedy
Founder of Threads of Hope Ministry, a writing and speaking ministry. CoAuthor of *Heart Friends*

We stand in the shallows, holding this book, hesitant to get more than our feet wet. Because diving into an in-depth, I'm-over-my-head Bible study of Ephesians is a scary endeavor. But as soon as we open the pages of *Dive Deeper: Finding Deep Faith Beyond Shallow Religion*, we hear Jenifer's friendly voice calling, "Come on in, the water's great! You can do this!" Through her expert guidance, compelling personal stories, and unique d.i.v.e. method of Bible study, Jenifer inspires us to dive into God's Word and dares us to move from a life of shallow religion to living in the transformation of a deeper faith. Dare to dive with Jenifer—the water is great!

—**Linda Crawford**
   Author of *Finding Balance* and *A Taste of Freedom Bible Studies*; contributing author of *Comforting Women in Crisis*

If you don't want to run the risk of being overwhelmed and drenched by the waves of God's grace and faithfulness, then don't read this book. In *Dive Deeper*, Jenifer Jernigan beckons us to explore beyond the comfortable and familiar surface to discover the depths of God's character as revealed in His Word. Plumb the depths of the book of Ephesians and develop the skills to study the Bible for yourself. It's not for the faint of heart but for those who desire faithful hearts.

—**Heather Zempel**
   Author of *Sacred Roads*, *Community is Messy*, and *Amazed and Confused*, Discipleship Pastor at National Community Church

DIVE
DEEPER

DIVE
DEEPER

finding deep faith
beyond shallow religion

JENIFER JERNIGAN

THOMAS NELSON
Since 1798

NASHVILLE   DALLAS   MEXICO CITY   RIO DE JANEIRO

Published in Nashville, Tennessee, by Thomas Nelson. Thomas Nelson is a trademark of HarperCollins Christian Publishing, Inc.

Page design and layout: Crosslin Creative
Images: istockphoto.com, vectorstock.com

Unless otherwise noted, Scripture quotations are taken from *The Voice*™ translation. © 2012 Ecclesia Bible Society. Used by permission. All rights reserved.

Note: Italics in quotations from *The Voice* are used to "indicate words not directly tied to the dynamic translation of the original language" but that "bring out the nuance of the original, assist in completing ideas, and . . . provide readers with information that would have been obvious to the original audience" (*The Voice*, preface). Emphasis in quotations from *The Voice* is indicated with the use of **boldface** type.

Author is represented by The Blythe Daniel Agency.

Thomas Nelson, Inc., titles may be purchased in bulk for educational, business, fund-raising, or sales promotional use. For information, please e-mail SpecialMarkets@ ThomasNelson.com.

Unless otherwise indicated,

Scripture quotations marked NKJV are taken from the NEW KING JAMES VERSION. © 1982 by Thomas Nelson, Inc. Used by permission. All rights reserved.

Scripture quotations designated "Amplified Bible" are taken from The Amplified Bible: Old Testament. ©1962, 1964 by Zondervan (used by permission); and from THE AMPLIFIED BIBLE: NEW TESTAMENT. © 1958 by the Lockman Foundation (used by permission).

Scripture quotations marked MSG are taken from *The Message* by Eugene H. Peterson. © 1993, 1994, 1995, 1996, 2000. Used by permission of NavPress Publishing Group. All rights reserved.

Scripture quotations marked NASB are taken from the NEW AMERICAN STANDARD BIBLE®, © The Lockman Foundation 1960, 1962, 1963, 1968, 1971, 1972, 1973, 1975, 1977, 1995. Used by permission.

Scripture quotations marked NIV are taken from the Holy Bible, New International Version®, NIV®. Copyright © 1973, 1978, 1984, 2011 by Biblica, Inc.™ Used by permission of Zondervan. All rights reserved worldwide. *www.zondervan.com*.

Scripture quotations marked NLT are taken from *Holy Bible*, New Living Translation. © 1996, 2004, 2007. Used by permission of Tyndale House Publishers, Inc., Carol Stream, Illinois 60188. All rights reserved.

Scripture quotations marked ESV are taken from THE ENGLISH STANDARD VERSION. © 2001 by Crossway Bibles, a division of Good News Publishers. All rights reserved.

ISBN: 9781401679217

Printed in the United States of America

14 15 16 17 18 19 RRD 6 5 4 3 2

For my husband,
You have loved me deeply, purely, and
sacrificially and because of that, I now
understand Christ's love for me.
I love you with all my heart.

Husbands, you must love your wives so *deeply, purely,
and sacrificially that we can understand it only when we*
compare it to the love the Anointed One has for His
bride, the church. Ephesians 5:25, The Voice

Contents

Introduction

A Diving Deeper Bible Study

 Mrs. Margaret came to me after Sunday morning worship, gently touched my arm, and said in her most lovely Southern accent, "Honey, you gotta get in the Word so you can do this thang for the Lord. Start studying and learning who God is; He wants you to know Him more."

I wanted to know God more, and I wanted to be BFFs with Jesus. I wanted to fall in love with the Scriptures and do whatever "thang" it was God wanted me to do. I wanted to experience a life transformed, but I had no idea what to do or where to start. How was I supposed to *study* the Bible? Did I need to sit, be quiet, and wait for God to proclaim some great revelation to me? Was I supposed to go out and buy commentaries and concordances? Should I start reading in the Old Testament or the New Testament? Did I need to enroll in seminary (again)?

I did the only logical thing I knew to do; I went to the store and bought a really cute notebook, a pen, and a pink highlighter. The next morning I got up very early, fixed a cup of coffee, grabbed my Bible, cute new notebook, pen, and highlighter, and sat down at my kitchen table.

I waited.

I flipped through the pages of my Bible, hoping something would jump out at me. Nothing. Then I remembered something I'd learned years earlier—a verse found in the book of Matthew.

"Ask, and it will be given to you; seek, and you
will find; knock, and it will be opened to you."

-Matthew 7:7 (NKJV)

I quickly turned to Matthew 7 and highlighted verse 7 in pink.
I opened my new notebook, grabbed my pen, and as tears began to
stream down my face, I wrote . . .

Um, God? I'm just going to assume You're listening to me. Can I
ask You a question? OK, thanks! I really, really, REALLY want
to know more about You. And, I really want to study my Bible
like Mrs. Margaret said I should. But, well . . . the thing is . . .
I don't know how. I mean, I've been in church all my life. I went
to Sunday school. And I went to vacation Bible school every
summer. I prayed the sinner's prayer and was baptized when I was
seven. I can say all the books of the Bible. My dad is a preacher.
Oh, and I went to Bible college. But I guess You know all that,
huh? You see . . . I know a lot about You. But, well . . . I don't
know You. And I want to. I really, really want to!! So here's my
question . . . can You teach me You? Like, everything about You?
Like, from beginning to end? Like, all there is to know? 'Cause
You see, here's the deal . . . I'm desperate. I am desperately in
need of You in my life. So, I'm asking, from the depths of my
heart, teach me? I want to know You. I NEED to know You.

(an excerpt from my journal, December 2002)

I laid my head down and began to cry. I desperately wanted Jesus to teach me Himself. I wanted the deep things of God, not the shallow religion I'd always settled for. My weeping turned quiet, and in those silent moments I heard a whisper in my heart: *"Yes. Yes, I will teach you Me."*

And teach me He has, calling me out of darkness into His glorious light to live abundantly, not to settle. Pulling me closer to His side, where I'm safe and protected, happy and whole. Challenging me to dive deeper, reach farther, and press harder into intimacy with Him. Opening wide the living and active Word, implanting it deep within my soul.

This book you hold in your hands is what I pray will be a tool to equip you to dive deeper into the living and active Word of God. Words that will speak Jesus' truth into your heart. Stories that will teach you and encourage you to press harder into Jesus and trust His unchanging Word. Questions and answers that will rustle your feathers and cause you to seek His truth all the more. Challenges that will push you and stretch you and lead you from the shallowness of religion to deep, lasting faith in Jesus.

d.i.v.e.
SATISFIED

 She was satisfied playing in a puddle. Sitting in the hole she'd dug in the snow-white beach sand, my daughter played for hours while others jumped waves and dove deep into the crystal blue waters. Every now and then the inside of her puddle would drain empty, and with yellow pail in hand, she'd walk to the ocean's edge. Cautiously, she would bend her small-framed body, holding tightly to that yellow pail, as the two of them met the rolling waves. Once her pail was full of salty, cool water, she'd wander back to her hand-made beach playground and turn the pail upside down. The insides of her sandy hole would instantly transform into a shallow puddle of ocean water.

Until it emptied once again.

The knock came at the door, and I opened it to find a pastor's wife, a churchgoing woman, and a Sunday school teacher all wrapped up in one, standing on my welcome mat. Her eyes were empty, her heart confused, her soul searching for more.

We sat at my dining room table late that Thursday night. Our coffee cups remained full, while the house remained empty. I watched the clock as minutes passed: first five, then ten, up to twenty.

The silence was finally broken as the heart's desire of this precious woman spilled forth through her words and tears. Her fingers tap-danced on the table, her voice pleading, as she asked, "Is God's

Word for me? I mean, is the Bible for *me*? Can it work for me? All my life I've heard its stories, memorized its verses. My parents always took me to church. I'm a pastor's wife, for cryin' out loud! But on the inside I feel numb. So disconnected. So . . . like the Bible is just another book. I need to know. Is this book for me?"

She was empty.

I smiled. I'd felt her pain. I'd known the longings of her heart, the need to know if the Bible and God had any worth for my life. I reached across the table, took her by the hand, lifted her head so that I could see into her eyes, and excitedly replied, "YES! Oh, yes, yes, yes! God's Word is for YOU. It can work for YOU. He is for YOU. And He longs for you to know Him more through the pages of His life-changing Word."

My daughter and this precious pastor's wife found themselves in what I like to call "puddle living," standing in the shallows but longing for the deep. One was satisfied to make her way to the ocean's edge when the inside of her puddle drained dry; the other was fearfully searching for answers while filling her pail with churchgoing and serving, and being who and what everyone expected the pastor's wife to be. But unlike my little girl, the pastor's wife was empty on the inside, living incomplete and fearful on the outside, needing her world turned upside down in a Jesus kind of way.

I've lived there too, inside that puddle that always drains dry.

I'm a church girl, a PK (preacher's kid). I don't remember a time in all my years of living under my parents' roof that I wasn't in church. Sunday school, Wednesday night prayer meetings, GA's, Acteens, youth group, summer camps, VBS, Bible drills, and on and on the list could grow. I grew up knowing all things church: the lingo, the traditions, the do's and the don'ts. Knowing the Bible, its stories and characters, was a must in my home. But what I failed to know on a personal, intimate level was the God of the Bible, and how He desired, more than anything, to transform me from the inside out. With each venture to church, my head filled with more and more knowledge but my heart was numb to relationship with Jesus. I had no idea how to dive into Scripture, how to connect to the heart of God through the pages of His Word. I ate what I was fed and lived the first fifteen-plus years of my Christian life on the regurgitated messages of others.

Yes, my head was full of Jesus stories, but the deep places of my heart were empty, craving more. Years ago I made the choice to dive deeper into God's Word because I needed some Jesus—not religion, or tradition, or denominational mandates. I just needed Jesus and His Word. I'm not going to lie to you. Diving deeper into the Scriptures has been one of the hardest things I've ever done. I'm no academic scholar. (And if you were to ask my second, third, or tenth grade English teachers, they'd have told you I'd never amount to much in life because I was "challenged" and had "learning disabilities.") I don't do well with big words. I'm very literal, yet I over-analyze everything. And I'm horrible at memorizing Scripture. But I haven't given up or given in, and I'm not going to.

Listen: I don't know where you are right now in your relationship with Jesus or your desire to dive deeper into His Word. But I'm almost certain you fall into one of these categories:

- Satisfied. You're satisfied and settled in your "church world," dipping into God's Word every now and then. Christian books and TV evangelists are your go-to's when life becomes a little shaky. Tuesday morning Bible study or Thursday night small group is your Jesus fill-up. Keeping the coffee station running on Sunday morning is your weekly service. You're satisfied, but emptiness looms.

- Afraid, yet searching. You fear the Bible and question whether or not it can work for you. You're trying your best to live up to what others think you are or should be. You tiptoe around the Scriptures because you're unsure how to dive in deep. Your heart longs for more. You desire intimacy with Jesus and a life lived abundantly; you just don't know where to go from here.

- Numb. You're numb to the things of God. Nothing about the Bible fazes you; it's the same ol', same ol'. You wish people would get over themselves, with all their Jesus stories and church talk, and leave you the heck alone. You have a past full of crap that you believe Jesus can't do anything with, and if one more person tells you that "God can take your mess and make a message out of it," you're going to slap him.

> We can't understand the deep things of God unless we're willing to go to the deep places with Him.

Friend, I've been satisfied, afraid, searching, and numb (sometimes I find myself still hanging out there). I get it! And because I get it, I'm here to help you dive in deep. I'm praying your satisfied heart becomes unsettled, your fearful heart experiences God's peace, your searching heart finds the answers it's looking for, and your numb heart becomes awakened to God's love and desire for you. God longs to change you from the inside out through His life-transforming Word. He longs to lead you from the shallows to the deep because we can't understand the deep things of God unless we're willing to go to the deep places with Him. So grab your swimsuit and let's dive in deeper.

WHERE DO WE BEGIN?

Making the choice to dive deeper into the Bible begins with believing that God's Word is more than just a book. Studying the Scriptures begins with understanding that they're meant to transform one's life from the inside out and deepen one's relationship with Jesus Christ.

All of Scripture is God-breathed; *in its* inspired *voice, we hear* useful teaching, rebuke, correction, *instruction, and* training for a life that is right so that God's people may be up to the task ahead and have all they need to accomplish every good work.

–2 Timothy 3:16-17

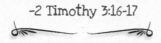

What Does It Mean to Study the Bible?

Head knowledge and fact-finding aren't the goal!

Studying the Bible is about:

- being able to know God fully and not just know about Him

- being able to experience His life-changing power actively working in your life

- knowing how to open His Word and understand it for yourself instead of living on the regurgitated messages of someone else.

Now let's talk about the how-to . . .

How to d.i.v.e. deeper into Studying the Bible

Pray. Ask the Lord what it is He wants you to study. It could be a particular book of the Bible, a certain passage of Scripture, a specific biblical character, verses related to an area in life where you seem to be struggling, and so forth.

Gather the tools needed to dive deeper into God's Word (see Appendix I for a list of other tools):

- a Bible

- a notebook or computer to record thoughts and discoveries

- pens and highlighters
- an English dictionary and *Strong's Exhaustive Concordance*
- commentaries or Bible software

With all the Bible translations available, how do you choose the best one for study purposes? For the in-depth study of the Scriptures we'll be doing in *Dive Deeper: Finding Deep Faith Beyond Shallow Religion*, I recommend a formal equivalence paired with a contextual equivalence translation. This study is written based on *The Voice* and the New King James Version, but you'll notice I use a number of other translations also: NLT, NASB, NIV, MSG, and ESV. Spend some time in a bookstore, reading several different translations, and choose one you're comfortable with. (See Appendix II.)

My favorite tools:

The John MacArthur Study Bible

Strong's Exhaustive Concordance

Expositor's Bible Commentary series

Holman Bible Dictionary

biblegateway.com

Get to know your Bible. We live in the technology age. With the use of Facebook, Twitter, blogs, Google+, Kindles, iPads, iPhones, and so forth, comes hours of figuring out how it all works: the functions, features, and purposes of each. The same is true with God's Word. When we begin to study the Bible, we must know and understand how to use each part. Throughout this study you'll be encouraged to d.i.v.e. deeper into the Scriptures using the different parts of your Bible: table of contents, book introductions, chapter divisions, cross-references, translation notes, study notes, and topical index. (See Appendix III.)

As we study, we'll also be investigating passages in various books of the Bible, so I want you to think of the Bible as a library of God's stories to His people, about His people, for the purpose of making known His plan to rescue a lost world through His Son, Jesus.

This library of stories is made up of sixty-six books—thirty-nine Old Testament books and twenty-seven New Testament books—written by forty authors over a period of sixteen hundred years.

Dive in. Here's where we dive in with both feet, my friend. This dive isn't going to be easy. You may flail about and gasp for breath. You may doggie-paddle your way around the Scriptures for a while, and it's possible, at times, that you may feel as though you're drowning. But believe me when I tell you, you can do this! You're going to learn to swim. You're going to learn to kick your feet and hold your breath, and before long you'll be doing the backstroke through the pages of God's Word!

> Formal equivalence, also known as a literal or word-for-word translation, seeks to retain the form of the Hebrew or Greek while producing basically understandable English.

In *Dive Deeper* we dive deep into the book of Ephesians. In each section you'll be guided through a number of verses and encouraged to use the d.i.v.e. format. The beauty of this format is that it goes beyond this study; it can be used anytime you desire to dive deeper into the Scriptures.

d.i.v.e.

define • investigate • visualize • embrace

The book of Ephesians is made up of six chapters, reflected in the six sections of this book. If we tried to study through a chapter a day, we'd drown. To make this d.i.v.e. manageable for us all, we're going to work through a few verses at a time, filling in and adding to the d.i.v.e. form found at the beginning of each lesson as we go.

Before I explain the d.i.v.e. method, please know that this is simply a beach tote full of tools to help you dive deeper into God's Word. We won't use them in a certain order, or use every tool equally. Use the pieces that work for you. In the first few passages we study, you may choose to work through only one portion of d.i.v.e., gradually adding more as we go; or you may choose to only read through my notes. For me, d.i.v.e. was once a method, a process, steps to follow in studying the Bible, but now it's a part of who I am and how I interact with God's Word. I pray the same will become true for you!

Here's how to d.i.v.e.:

d. (define)

As you read through the text . . .

- write down words. Specifically, write down any repeated, long, unusual, and unfamiliar words and phrases. Use an English dictionary and/or a *Strong's Concordance* to define these key words. If you're comfortable writing/marking in your Bible, consider underlining or highlighting these key words; for those who'd rather not mark in their Bibles, try printing the passage you're studying in the version of your choice. You can find a number of Bible translations on biblegateway.com.

define tip: The Old Testament was written in Hebrew and Aramaic, and the New Testament was written in Greek. Although scholars have done their best to stay as close to the original text as possible, some of the richness of the languages have been lost. Defining these words, especially using a *Strong's Concordance*, allows us to take English words and uncover their original meaning.

As we break down verses from each chapter, I'll pull out a number of key words that we'll study together. I encourage you to also pull out your own words and define them.

i. (investigate)

To investigate each passage, we'll ask questions. Who? What? When? Where? Why? How? (See Appendix IV.)

As you investigate verses . . .

Have you ever heard the word *exegete*, or perhaps *exegetical*? These words simply refer to investigating verses one by one.

- understand the context. Although every word of the Bible has been given to us by God, the Bible wasn't written directly to us. When seeking to understand the context, we must look at the entire paragraph or thought, as well as the history, cultural setting, and geography of the day.

- use cross-references. Scripture is the best examiner of itself, so use cross-references to investigate what other Scriptures have to say about the passages you're studying. Zoom out to see the bigger picture, to gain better clarity on what is happening in the passage.

- use commentaries. Get a better grasp on the thoughts you may not completely understand by reading the comments of experts who have studied the Scripture. (See Appendix I.)

Everything written in the days of old was recorded to give us instructions *for living*. We find encouragement through the Scriptures and a call to perseverance that will produce hopeful living.

–Romans 15:4

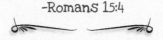

As we break down verses from each chapter, I'll ask a number of investigative questions. I encourage you to ask your own questions and search hard for the answers.

v. (visualize)

- Visualize content. Start by taking a "snapshot" of the whole chapter by reading it through at least three times so you understand the big picture (often referred to as the *context* of the passage).

- Make an outline or paraphrased summary of the content. This helps you think through the content and organization of the text, which helps you understand its meaning.

visualize tip: In visualizing passages of Scripture, break down the verse based upon the placement of commas and punctuation marks.

I encourage you to make your own outline, with a brief description for each section. Make this outline as detailed or as simple as you'd like it to be.

e. (embrace)

As you investigate the Scriptures . . .

- embrace learning. How has your way of thinking about life, others, and God been challenged? Are there areas of your life where you need to step from the shallows into the deep? Obeying what we've been taught is the final piece, and it's very important that we not walk away until we've asked the question, *Jesus, what are You challenging me to live more deeply?* Remember, our goal in studying the Bible is connecting with the heart of God on personal, intimate levels and living out what He's spoken to us, so don't leave out this step. We can do the hard work of defining, investigating, and visualizing the passage but stop short of embracing it, and making it a part of who we are.

- embrace WOWs (Words of Wisdom). Write, draw, paint, or create a Word of Wisdom visual from the chapter or section of Scripture you've studied as a reminder to embrace God's challenge and truth. (See Appendix V.)

Put the word into action. If you think hearing is what matters most, you are going to find you have been deceived.

–James 1:22

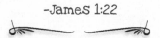

Friend, I want to promise you a few things before we d.i.v.e. into Ephesians:

- God will meet you on the pages of Scripture, and He'll teach you Himself.

- The Holy Spirit, your internal Teacher, will open your eyes, heart, and mind and give you the wisdom and knowledge to know how to apply His Word to your life.

- God will transform your life from the inside out and move you beyond the shallows of religion into deeper faith in Him as you study His Word and come to know Him more.

I am before the throne for you! You can do this! Work hard and finish well! Now, let's d.i.v.e. deeper into the Word together!

In Him

EPHESIANS ONE

d.i.v.e. into LESSON ONE

d. (define.)

i. (investigate.)

v. (visualize.)

e. (embrace)

An Unlikely Becomes Extraordinary

Ephesians 1:1-2

 Before you begin your time of study and learning, spend a few moments in prayer asking God to give you an open heart and mind to learn new truths from His Word.

 ## v. (visualize)

Take a snapshot of Ephesians 1 by reading through the chapter at least three times so you understand the big picture. As you're reading, make note of any verse(s) that tugs at your heart; this may be the WOW God wants you to embrace from chapter 1.

In this lesson we're going to zoom in on Ephesians 1:1–2. As you read these verses again, begin to d.i.v.e. below the surface, jotting down words, asking questions, and outlining or paraphrasing the text. To help you get started, I've included my d.i.v.e. for Ephesians 1:1–2. In the lessons to come, I encourage you to open your beach tote and use the d.i.v.e. tools as they work for you, filling in the blank d.i.v.e. form as you go. Remember: we won't use the tools in a certain order, or use every one equally. In the first few passages we study,

3

you may choose to work through only one portion of d.i.v.e., gradually adding more as we go; or you may choose to only read through my notes.

d. (define)

emissary
will of God
saints
grace
peace
in Christ (NKJV)

i. (investigate)

Who is the author of this letter?
What is Paul's backstory?
Why did Paul write Ephesians?
Why was Ephesus so special to Paul?
When and from where did Paul write?
Under whose authority does Paul write, serve, and minister?
From where do grace and peace come?

v. (visualize)

Ephesians 1:1–2. Paul's greeting.

e. (embrace)

Ephesians 1:1–2 reminds me that God takes the unlikely and makes them extraordinary. My jaded past, full of regrets and hurts, rejections and losses, is a canvas upon which God desires to create a beautiful life masterpiece evidenced by the reality that He has gifted me with grace and flooded my life with peace.

ARE YOU READY? LET'S D.I.V.E. INTO EPHESIANS!

 i. (investigate)

 Read Ephesians 1:1. Who claims authorship of this letter?

_____

 Who was Paul?

_____

Paul was chosen by God to be "an emissary of Jesus the Anointed, *directly commissioned as His representative* by the will of God." He passionately embraced his calling and cherished the message behind that calling, to make Christ known. However, he hadn't always been zealous about making Christ known. In fact, he'd been adamantly against Christ and all things pertaining to Christianity.

Born in the Roman city of Tarsus, he was given the name Saul (a Jewish name) at birth, a name most likely chosen in honor of Israel's King Saul of the Old Testament. Later in life, Saul would come to be known predominantly by his Roman name, Paul (Acts 13:9). Being raised in a Jewish home meant Paul was well versed in Jewish Scriptures and followed strictly the traditions of his religion. At a young age he was sent to synagogue, where he learned to read and write by copying passages from the Old Testament texts. From the same Old Testament Scriptures he also learned the Hebrew language. At home he learned Aramaic, and out in the community he learned Greek. As was customary for every Jewish boy, Paul was expected to learn a trade, a skill that would be useful to him later in life. From Acts 18:3, we learn Paul's chosen trade was tent making.

Scholars believe that sometime between age thirteen to eighteen, Paul left his hometown and went to Jerusalem, where he studied under the rabbi Gamaliel (Acts 22:3). Gamaliel was thought to be the greatest Jewish teacher of his day, and under the influence of his teaching, Paul wrote, "I excelled in the teachings of Judaism far above other Jewish leaders, and I was zealous to practice the ways of our ancestors" (Galatians 1:14). Paul not only pronounced himself zealous to practice the ways of his ancestors; he also acknowledged himself to be a Pharisee (Philippians 3:5).

It's at the stoning of Stephen, the first Christian martyr, where Paul, still referred to as Saul, is first introduced in Scripture.

Read Acts 7:57–58. Describe the scene.

Pharisee means "the separated ones." Pharisees believed that the only way to God was through the law. They were lovers of tradition and were extreme rule followers.

Saul was puddle living; he'd made his home in the shallows. He stood there on the day of Stephen's death as a man well learned in tradition, religion, and the law. He had much intellectual knowledge of the Jesus Stephen preached, and he knew a great deal about the move of Christianity sweeping across the land. What Saul failed to grasp, though, from all his learning, was the Man behind the movement. Saul's head was filled with knowledge over the years, yet his heart remained empty and calloused toward God and His love for him. He continued to deny Christ as the Messiah and was dumbfounded by the idea that God desired a personal, intimate relationship with him.

Saul consented to Stephen's death and continued to persecute the young Christian church in Jerusalem, forcing many of those believers to scatter abroad. His zealous hatred for Christ drove him to go "on a rampage—hunting the church, house after house, dragging both men and women to prison" (Acts 8:3).

Read Acts 9:1–2. Describe Saul's behavior. Who was he adamantly against? For what reason did Saul go to the high priest? What was his ultimate goal?

_____

_____

_____

A LIFE PLUNGED INTO THE DEEP

I'm sure he didn't expect anything out of the ordinary to happen that day. Saul got up that morning, ate breakfast, packed everything he'd need, prepared the donkeys for the weeklong journey, readied his traveling companions, and headed to Damascus. His mission: to arrest and put in prison anyone who proclaimed Jesus Christ as Lord and Savior.

Read Acts 9:3–6. As Saul got nearer to Damascus, what out-of-the-ordinary event occurred? Describe the scene.

_____

_____

_____

I have no doubt this was one of those "shut-the-front-door!" moments in Saul's life. Can you even imagine what took place? Saul, his heart beating faster and faster the closer he gets to Damascus. The persecution of Christian believers, the dragging them out of their homes and throwing them in prison, is like a drug to him. He is eager for the high he's about to experience from the first "catch" of the day. BUT, in the presence of Jesus Christ, Saul is driven face to the ground. The voice of Christ rings loudly in his ears. It is stern, power-filled, authoritative, demanding of respect and awe. And yet, at the same time, Christ's voice overflows with love, spills forth with grace, and reveals a yearning for this knowledge-driven man to fall head over heels in love with Him.

Saul's life was based on traditions of the past, filled with religious rituals and checklists of how-tos and how-not-tos. He'd learned to live his life according to the law, dotting all the *i*'s and crossing all the *t*'s. On this day, however, everything he'd learned, all he'd been taught, when held up to the light of the presence of Jesus Christ, was unseen, poured out, drained dry. His knowledge no longer amounted to anything. Tradition was erased. Religious rituals were no longer practiced. The checklists of how-tos and how-not-tos were lost forever.

> The voice of God is stern. It is power-filled. It is authoritative. It is demanding of respect and awe.

As he lay facedown on the ground, Saul heard a voice unlike any he'd ever heard. Just as he was smack-dab in the middle of his sin, Christ called Saul out, spoke his name, and questioned his actions.

"Who are You, Lord?" Saul asked with enough wits about him to recognize the voice as one of power and authority. I can't help but wonder if he cringed and held his breath as those words left his lips. Or did he dig his fingers deep into that dirt road, grasping for something tangible to hold on to?

Whether his body cringed, the breath escaped his lungs, or he searched for an anchor to secure himself to, I'm almost certain that his "shut-the-front-door!" turned into an "I'm toast!" when the words "I am Jesus . . ." reached his ears.

Jesus. He knew Jesus. He'd learned about this Man his entire life. He was familiar with the stories and each character that played an active part. He also knew how to flip any conversation with a Jesus follower, causing that unwitting soul to doubt what he believed. He knew it all, yet he knew absolutely nothing.

His ears ringing and his mind now swirling with the words, "I am Jesus . . . ," his heart could no longer play silent partner. Saul had left his home days earlier, prepared and enthusiastic to arrest any Christian he could find. But in this moment, it was Saul who'd been captured. His heart had been captured by the truth: that he'd been imprisoned all his life to rules and regulations, perceptions and expectations. The truth that he really knew nothing of who Jesus truly was. The truth that he needed to step forward from his life of shallow living into one of deeper faith in Jesus..

Saul was instantly smitten by Christ's love for him. He was blanketed by God's magnificent grace. He was rocked to his core, and life as he knew it was turned upside down. In response, he immediately asked the Lord, "What do You want me to do?" His thoughts, his plans, his desires no longer existed. Humbly, he submitted himself to the lordship of Christ in his life.

Years passed, and Saul came to be known as the apostle Paul, a great defender of the faith. His passion for God and his willingness to do whatever God called him to do led him from place to place, house to house, synagogue to synagogue—and prison to prison.

 ### i. (investigate)

When and from where did Paul write this letter?

_____

_____

Being an emissary, a messenger of the Gospel, wasn't easy or safe, and often afforded one the opportunity to rustle the feathers of those in charge of rule following and tradition keeping. Jesus followers who spoke openly and freely about Christ's love, forgiveness, and acceptance of all were often accused of wrongs they hadn't committed and forced to serve time for "crimes" that were made up in

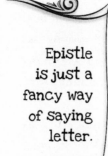

the minds of the powers that be. As a result of those very things, we find Paul imprisoned under house arrest in Rome when he penned this letter.

Epistle is just a fancy way of saying letter.

His crime? Paul had been arrested in Jerusalem, accused of bringing a Gentile believer into areas of the Jewish temple that were forbidden places for any Gentile to enter (Acts 21:28).

Imprisoned physically? Yes. Bound spiritually? Not at all. Paul was able to endure his physical imprisonment because he'd been set free from the bondage of sin.

Because Paul penned this letter during his first Roman imprisonment, this epistle is known as one of Paul's four prison epistles, Philippians, Colossians, and Philemon being the others. All of the prison epistles can be dated between AD 60 and 62.

i. (investigate)

Why did Paul write this letter, and who were its intended recipients?

_____

_____

_____

_____

The phrase "in Ephesus" isn't included in many of the early manuscripts. So who were Paul's intended recipients? Scholars believe Paul meant for this letter to be circulated among the churches of Asia Minor, the church of Ephesus possibly being the first stop, hence the titling of this letter "Ephesians."

The city of Ephesus held a special place in Paul's heart. He spent three years there, teaching, discipling, and ministering (Acts 19–20). He'd invested emotionally, spiritually, and physically into the lives of the believers there. Paul meant for this letter to encourage them to continue loving God and their brothers and sisters in Christ unconditionally and without reserve.

Encouragement wasn't Paul's only purpose. It was also his hope and prayer that his words would further help believers understand the importance of their relationship in Christ over a life of tradition and rule following. Many had been taught that following rules and acting out rituals would make them accepted in God. Paul knew firsthand this wasn't the case. He knew that living deep faith was an overflow of one's position in Christ. He wasn't out to offer shallow religion, filled with perceptions, expectations, and regulations; his desire was to open the door of relationship with God and between individuals.

> Living deep faith is an overflow of one's position in Christ.

Paul paints a picture of what the church, the body of Christ—His hands, His feet, His heartbeat—should be. Diverse, yet unified. Bold, yet compassionate. Christ-centered, not me-centered. Broken and poured out for the lost, hurting, and lonely. Loving on the widow and the orphan, the homeless and the prisoner. Doing life with the stripper, the drug addict, the gay or lesbian neighbor. Chatting, grappling, and searching for answers with those wondering what the heck life is all about. Looking past the piercings, the tats, and the masks that hide, into the heart of the person. Accepting people where they are, realizing none of us are any better than the others. He paints the picture and challenges the church to live life deep as the extension of God's nature, His character, His person.

 e. (embrace)

God took an unlikely and made him extraordinary. He knew what Saul was and He knew *who* Saul was. He knew the makeup of Saul's heart, its hatred, bitterness, and pride. God knew the venomous words Saul spoke against Christ followers and the evil plans he had set in motion. Yet, He saw past all of Saul's unlikeliness and into the heart of the man Paul, knowing exactly what He could make Saul into. God knew that inside Saul, sin and all, was someone great.

> A Gentile is any person who isn't of Jewish descent.

Saul was chosen and appointed to take the message of the saving power of the Gospel of Jesus Christ to the lost, specifically, the lost Gentiles. He became as passionate about sharing Christ as he'd once been about persecuting others for their belief in Him. Saul wasn't a likely pick for one who could be used of God. Based on his background and according to the world's standards for those who "deserve" God's favor, he wasn't even in the lineup. But it's so like God to take the unlikeliest of people, the ordinary, run-of-the-mill individuals, and make them into extraordinary men and women of God—extraordinary only because it's God who works from the inside out to accomplish the mission at hand. It's God who transforms and sanctifies and leads us from the shallows to the deep. And it's God who empowers and enables those He chooses to deeply live out the task He's set before them.

 Do you feel like an unlikely candidate to be used by God? What circumstances, past or present, do you feel hinder God from giving you an extraordinary testimony?

_____

_____

_____

If you're anything like me, you have a long list of "circumstances" staring back at you. You're probably scanning it from top to bottom, confirming in your mind what you already thought to be true . . . *Yep, with all this crap in my life, there's no way God can use me for anything at all, much less anything extraordinary.* I want you to understand something: those "circumstances" we've just written down don't hinder God from working in us and through us. We hinder God from doing extraordinary things in our lives because of our disobedience and refusal to hand over to Him all our unlikeliness.

That may sound harsh, and you may be saying to yourself, *She has no idea what's happened to me. She doesn't understand my pain or know my secrets.* You're right. I don't know what's happened to you, I don't understand your exact pain, and I don't know your secrets. But I know my pain, my secrets, and the deep wounds I've lived through, and I know their crippling effects.

I also know we can step forward into freedom. Is it easy? Hardly! But, we can stand in the midst of a present circumstance and not be defined by it. We can, but we must choose to. We must choose to not let it hinder us from being extraordinary for God.

Whatever our past life experiences or present circumstances, God desires to take them all and fashion them into something absolutely beautiful for Him. He wants to transform us from the inside out, making us into extraordinary men and women who have a passion to know Him more and make Him known in our day. Why? Because it's His will and His good pleasure to do such a thing.

PEACE FOLLOWS GRACE

Read Ephesians 1:2 in the New King James Version and fill in the blanks.

_____ to you and _____ from God our Father and the Lord Jesus Christ.

d. (define)

Based on your understanding right now of the word *grace*, define it in the space that follows. Don't look ahead for an answer. Don't rack your brain trying to come up with one, either. Just write down what you believe grace to be. And, if you don't have any idea, that's okay! If you can't seem to put your thoughts into words, try drawing a picture of "grace" in the margin.

_____

_____

Based on your current understanding of the word *peace*, define it in the space that follows. Again, don't look ahead for an answer or rack your brain trying to come up with one. Just write down what you believe peace to be. And as before, if you don't have any idea, that's okay! Try drawing a picture of "peace" instead.

_____

_____

Using a *Strong's Concordance*, look up the Greek terms for *grace* and *peace* as found in Ephesians 1:2. Record the definitions here.

See Appendix I for FREE online tools that contain a *Strong's Concordance*.

_____

_____

_____

_____

_____

d.i.v.e. DEEPER INTO GRACE AND PEACE.

Grace and peace. Simple words. Common words. Yet these two words carry a punch that's often overlooked. Growing up in the atmosphere of the church, I always heard grace defined as "God's riches at Christ's expense." The acrostic captured my attention each time I heard it spoken. These words strung together painted a beautiful picture in my mind of Christ's death on the cross, but I never really understood the depth of meaning in the five-letter word *grace*.

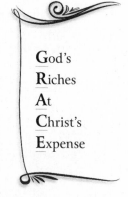

God's
Riches
At
Christ's
Expense

When peace was mentioned, it was often partnered with the phrase "that passes all under-standing." Again, a beautiful phrase; "a peace that passes all understanding" sounded so comforting and gave me warm fuzzies. But I didn't completely grasp its meaning either. Grace and peace. For me, these were just two more of the "churchy" words I often threw around in conversations. Sadly, I knew nothing of God's grace, nor had I experienced His peace that, supposedly, passes all understanding.

As Scripture has been translated over time from its original Hebrew (Old Testament) and Greek (New Testament), many of the rich meanings have been lost in our English language. One of the first things God led me to do when He captured my heart and began leading me beyond shallow religion into deeper faith was to dive deeper into His Word and discover the real meanings of the words on my "churchy word" list.

Grace was one of the first words I needed to understand. You looked up *grace* in *Strong's Concordance*; now let's look at the defini-tion of *grace* from a few other sources:

Thayer's Greek Definitions defines grace as:

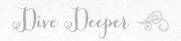

1) that which affords joy, pleasure, delight, sweetness, charm, loveliness: grace of speech; 2) good will, loving-kindness, favour, of the merciful kindness by which God, exerting his holy influence upon souls, turns them to Christ, keeps, strengthens, increases them in Christian faith, knowledge, affection, and kindles them to the exercise of the Christian virtues.[1]

Holman Bible Dictionary defines grace as:

an undeserved acceptance and love received from another, especially the characteristic attitude of God in providing salvation for sinners[2]

Using these as a guide, write your own personalized definition of grace.

_____

_____

_____

_____

Understanding what grace truly means was a pivotal moment for me. Here's my own personalized definition of grace:

Grace is a beautiful gift from God that I in no way deserve. God gave me this gift through His Son, Jesus Christ, whom I've received as the Lord and Savior of my life. Grace sets me free from the bondage of sin and enables me to live the life God created me to live.

Truly understanding grace opened the door for my being able to live in God's peace—a peace that does pass all understanding. Peace, you discovered from *Strong's Concordance*, is the Greek word *eiréné*. Let's look at the definition of peace from a few other sources:

Thayer's Greek Definitions defines peace as:

1) a state of national tranquility, exemption from the rage and havoc of war; 2) peace between individuals, i.e. harmony, concord[3]

Holman Bible Dictionary defines peace as:

well-being, restoration, reconciliation with God, and salvation in the fullest sense[4]

Using these as a guide, write your own personalized definition of peace.

_____

_____

_____

_____

Accepting God's peace and learning to live in the beauty of it changed my life. Here's my own personalized definition of peace:

God's peace, a result of His grace, dispels the war within my heart and mind. The chaos in my life that came from trying to live up to the perceptions and expectations of others was driven out as He restored me to Himself, quieting my heart and mind.

Paul very often paired the concepts of grace and peace together in his writings. Remember, he'd once been a persecutor of the church and opposed to all things Christianity. His heart, mind, and soul raged inside him as he tried desperately to follow all the rules. In his pursuit of dotting all the *i*'s and crossing all the *t*'s, a life of peace was far from his grasp. Paul understood full well that once a person received and accepted the undeserved gift of God's grace, he or she would also be filled with God's peace. Paul's embracing of God's grace opened the doors to a life of peace with the almighty God.

Read what he said in Titus 2.

We have cause to celebrate because the grace of God has appeared, offering *the gift of* salvation to all people. *Grace arrives* with its own instruction: run away from anything that leads us away from God; abandon the lusts and passions of this world; live life now in this age *with awareness* and self-control, doing the right thing and keeping yourselves holy. *Watch for His return;* expect the blessed hope *we all will share* when our great God and Savior, Jesus the Anointed, appears again. He gave His body for our sakes and will not only break us free from *the chains of* wickedness, but He will also prepare a community uncorrupted by the world that He would call His own—people who are passionate about doing the right thing.

-Titus 2:11-14

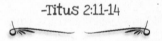

Do you see the grace and peace in these verses?

God's grace: "The grace of God has appeared, offering *the gift of* salvation to all people." Jesus Christ is God's grace in the flesh, appearing to everyone in order to bring them salvation.

God's peace: "He gave His body for our sakes and will [not only] break us free . . ." (Titus 2:14). God's peace is brought about through the redemptive work on the cross. Christ's death redeemed us, or freed us from the debt we owed because of our sin. His blood paid our ransom and restored us to peaceful fellowship with God.

Grace and peace. You can't have one without the other. Grace given by God. Peace made possible through the shed blood of Christ on the cross. Both undeserved by fallen humankind. But both poured out abundantly upon us because God desired relationship with the people He created. Grace greater than all our sins. Peace that passes all understanding.

Grace and peace. Far more than just two churchy words on a list, they encompass the beauty of God.

 e. (embrace)

What do God's grace and peace mean to you? Where would you be without them?

_____

_____

_____

_____

_____

d.i.v.e. into LESSON TWO

d. (define)

i. (investigate)

v. (visualize)

e. (embrace)

LESSON TWO

Let Me In!

Ephesians 1:3-14

 Before you begin your time of study and learning, spend a few moments in prayer asking God to give you an open heart and mind to learn new truths from His Word.

 ### v. (visualize)

Take a snapshot of Ephesians 1 by reading through the chapter at least three times, reminding yourself of the big picture. Is there a WOW you're embracing and implanting in your heart? Take a few moments to review that verse(s). Don't forget to add to your outline/paraphrase.

In this lesson we're going to zoom in on Ephesians 1:3–14. As you read these verses again, begin to d.i.v.e. below the surface.

IN CHRIST

It's human nature: we all want to be "in" in some form or fashion. We want to be a part of something beyond ourselves, and we all want to matter. I spent years pursuing "in-ness." I've been "in the know" about a lot of things, and I've spent my days as part of the "in crowd." I've found myself "in the right place at the right time" on a few occasions, but I've also found myself "in the *wrong* place at the wrong time." And being "in love"? That's a beast all its own. But with each experience of being "in," I still felt as though I didn't truly belong.

Not only did I desire to be "in"; I wanted to be significant. I wanted to matter. I wanted to have purpose and worth, and I wanted to be cherished. I searched for significance and purpose in boyfriends, friendships, eventually marriage, parenting, and religion. I tried to find my worth in others' perceptions of me, and because I'm a people pleaser by nature, I did things for people to gain their approval.

My desires and pursuits only led me down the dark road of pain, heartache, shame, and guilt. My life was a tangled web of chaos because I chose to do what I wanted to do and rejected God's Word. I was in control and literally dared God to step in. My sin left me void of relationship with Him and in a heap of trouble, completely hopeless.

If I had my guess, I'd say you want to feel significant too. You want to matter and have purpose and value. You've probably searched for significance in relationships, a job, or a situation, only to find yourself feeling less significant and worthless in the end. And on some level you probably have a tangled web of your own chaos and sin. I'm sure your sin has caused you, as it has me, to greatly lack in your relationship with God.

We have this longing and desire to be "in" something and feel significant because it's a longing God created deep within us. It's a place in our hearts and lives meant to be filled only by Him. And because God loves us so much and desires that we find our worth and purpose in Him, He woos us to Himself, making us "accepted in the Beloved" (Ephesians 1:6 NKJV)—accepted, redeemed, and forgiven because the grace of God sent Christ to the cross, destroying our tangled web of sin and making us one in Him.

e. (embrace)

What are some things you've desired to be "in"? Did being "in" those things make you feel as though you belonged? Did it give you worth and significance?

_____

_____

_____

_____

_____

Read Ephesians 1:3–14 in the New King James Version. How many times in these few verses does Paul use the phrase "in Christ," "in Him," and/or "in the Beloved"? _____

What do you think it means to be "in Christ"?

_____

_____

_____

_____

_____

In is synonymous with the word *unity*. Both words carry the idea of belonging, oneness, cohesion, togetherness. In this letter, Paul encouraged the saints (believers) of Asia Minor, as well as believers today, to be unified with Christ as individuals and as a church. He taught that as members of the church, each of us should be a vital part of a body that is busy about the mission of making Christ known.

But before we can join together as one body, one unit, one church, we must understand the importance of being made one in Christ.

Let's visit with the author of Genesis to understand the beginnings of our being created to be "in Christ."

AN APPRENTICESHIP

In Genesis 1:26 Moses recorded these words of God: "Let Us conceive *a new creation*—humanity—*made* in Our image, *fashioned* according to Our likeness."

It was on day six of creation that God the Father, God the Son, and God the Holy Spirit created humankind, those with whom They desired intimate relationship. The English word *image* is a translation of the Hebrew word *tselem* which is "from an unused root meaning to *shade.*"[1] Other Hebraists explain *tselem* to mean "an image as that which is a replica or shadow of the original."[2]

God created us to live in the realm of the shade or shadow He casts, a shade that reflects His nature and character. A shadow is positional; its placement is dependent upon the object of origin. Being created in the image of God means that He's positioned us to live in His shadow.

In order to step out in a leadership position in the church I attend, a person is required to spend one semester apprenticing under a current leader. During that apprenticeship, the apprentice is to shadow the leader, learning how he or she leads, loves, and serves. The leader pours into the apprentice's life, guiding, directing, and helping that person grow in the areas where God has gifted him or her. The two are a close pair during this time, in constant conversation as they do life and ministry together.

I think of my being created in the image of the triune God much like this apprenticeship. I'm to shadow Christ. To learn from Him. To mimic how He loves and serves others. To receive His guidance, direction, and help. To be in constant conversation with Him as we do life and ministry together. Positionally, I'm to be in His realm of safekeeping, His shadow, His shade.

Neither life's circumstances nor my emotions/feelings ever determine my position in Christ. My position as God's daughter, of living life from the shadow He casts, is based solely on His magnificent grace, which was freely given through Jesus Christ's death on the cross.

A HYMN OF PRAISE

In Ephesians 1:3–14, it's clear that Paul understood and embraced his position in Christ rather than his current situation of imprisonment. His living from "in Christ" is clearly reflected in this doxology. Paul opened with the words "Blessed be God . . ." better translated "[Praised be] God, the Father of our Lord Jesus the Anointed One, who grants us every spiritual blessing in these heavenly realms *where we live* in the Anointed."

A *doxology* is a hymn of praise.

God the Father isn't the only One Paul acknowledged in this time of worship. Just as God the Father, God the Son, and God the Holy Spirit were all actively present and working in our being created to shade or shadow God—to live in the realm of His safekeeping, mimicking and living out our lives from that position—so too are They all involved in our being made one in Christ and deserving of our worship.

🖋 **Reread Ephesians 1:3–14 in The New King James Version.**
Interact with the passage by completing the following activity.

For in God, in Christ, and in the Holy Spirit, we are . . .

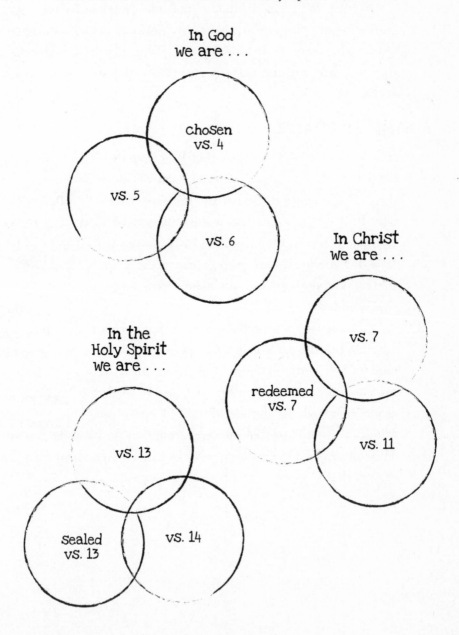

In God
we are . . .

chosen
vs. 4

vs. 5

vs. 6

In Christ
we are . . .

vs. 7

redeemed
vs. 7

vs. 11

In the
Holy Spirit
we are . . .

vs. 13

sealed
vs. 13

vs. 14

d.i.v.e. DEEPER INTO WHO YOU TRULY ARE

Read Ephesians 1:3–14 one more time, using the activity you just completed to d.i.v.e. deeper into these verses, making them personal to you. I've included my own personal example from each section and given you lines on which to jot down your thoughts, struggles, and the resolutions you came to as you dove deeper into these verses. If you haven't already done so, define unfamiliar words. Use cross-references to investigate what other Scriptures have to say about this passage. Consider reading these verses from another translation, like the New International Version.

in God the Father . . .
Take a moment and jot down what these verses mean in your life:

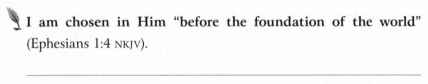 I am chosen in Him "before the foundation of the world" (Ephesians 1:4 NKJV).

_____

_____

_____

_____

We stood in a circle on the playground, nervously laughing, chatting, and looking over our shoulders. The boys stood, bowed up like a flock of banty roosters, strutting their masculine sixth grade stuff and talking among themselves. We knew exactly what they were deliberating.

Ben, taller than the rest and with dark-brown hair and sky-blue eyes, the most popular boy in the sixth grade, the one all the girls

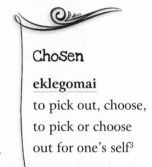

Chosen

eklegomai
to pick out, choose,
to pick or choose
out for one's self[3]

wanted to "go with," kept looking at me. I wanted so badly for him to choose me, but I was still fairly new to this school, and my friends' perms didn't make their hair frizzy, like mine did. They were allowed to wear makeup; I had to wait another year. They were skinny; I was on the fluffy side. And unlike mine (my dad was the "preacher-man"), their dads had normal jobs.

As the five boys turned around and began walking toward us, we broke open our circle and unfolded into a straight line, as if we were about to play Red Rover. But we all knew better.

My heart was racing, my hands were sweating, and I was silently praying Ben would choose me. Then everything would be right in my sixth grade world. We made eye contact—a sure sign, I thought—but within an arm's length, he shifted to his right. And chose the other girl. My heart shattered. Ben didn't choose me; no one chose me. I was the leftover sixth girl to those five boys.

"Not chosen" became a recurring theme in my life. Until Jesus.

I love *The Voice* translation of Ephesians 1:4: "God chose us to be in a relationship with Him even before He laid out plans for this world; He wanted us to live holy lives characterized by love, *free from sin*, and blameless before Him."

Before the foundation of the world, God chose me with my frizzy hair, fluffy body, no makeup, and preacher-man dad. He walked straight to me and called me by name because I was the one He wanted.

I am predestined to be adopted (Ephesians 1:5).

🖋 I am accepted in the Beloved (Ephesians 1:6).

_____

_____

_____

in God the Son . . .
Take a moment and jot down what these verses mean
in your life:

🖋 I am redeemed through the blood (Ephesians 1:7).

_____

_____

_____

God created me to live in Him. He chose me before the foundation of the world to experience a thriving, intimate relationship
with Him, but sin held me captive. I was its slave; it, my master.
For me to experience relationship with God, I had to be redeemed,
bought back from the one who held me captive.

Klyne Snodgrass says of redemption:

Redemption has its roots in the Old Testament idea of the covenant and in the language of the ancient marketplace; in both
instances it involved the idea of purchasing or buying back some
item or person that would otherwise be lost, taken prisoner, or
destroyed.

He goes on to say,

"Of the ten times 'redemption' occurs in the New Testament,
seven are in Paul's letters, three of these in Ephesians. Paul's

readers understood the word to signify release from bondage through the payment of a price. The price paid is clearly the 'blood' of Christ, which is merely a shorthand way of pointing to his sacrificial death and the new covenant it established with God."[4]

Redemption (apolutrōsis) as found in Ephesians 1:7 means

1) a releasing effected by payment of ransom,

1a) redemption, deliverance,

1b) liberation procured by the payment of a ransom.[5]

In the Old Testament, animals were slain and their blood offered on the altars of the tabernacle and temple. Although this was the system set in place at the time, the blood was never able or intended to cleanse the offender of his sin. These sacrificial animals were only substitutes for the Lamb that was to come, for our redemption "was not paid with things that perish (like silver and gold), but with the precious blood of the Anointed, who was like a perfect and unblemished sacrificial lamb. God determined to send Him before the world began, but He came *into the world* in these last days for your sake. Through Him, you've been brought to trust in God, who raised Him from the dead and glorified Him for the very reason that your faith and hope are in Him" (1 Peter 1:18–21).

The only acceptable payment for my sin debt was the shed blood of Christ. He is the One who redeemed me, releasing me from a life of bondage so that I could live free.

I am forgiven of sins (Ephesians 1:7).

🖋 I have obtained an inheritance (Ephesians 1:11).

_____

_____

_____

in God the Holy Spirit . . .
Take a moment and jot down what these verses mean
in your life:

🖋 I heard the word of truth, the gospel of my salvation (Ephesians
1:13).

_____

_____

_____

🖋 I am sealed with the Holy Spirit of promise (Ephesians 1:13).

_____

_____

_____

By God I am chosen. By Christ I am redeemed. And by the Holy
Spirit I am sealed and secure at the moment of my salvation.

When I was seven, I walked the aisle of our church during
the fall revival. I prayed the "sinners' prayer" and thus began my
Christian life—at least what I understood it to be. But that night
something else began, years of wondering, struggling, and teetering

back and forth on the salvation seesaw, asking the question, *Am I saved or am I not?*

My doubt was rooted in something I was told that fall night: "You're a Christian now, and Christians don't act that way. There are things you do and there are things you don't do." Those words were implanted deep in my head, and I began keeping close check on all the things I did. *Am I allowed to do that? Oh no! I did that. I must not be saved anymore.* It was a constant battle—one I could never seem to win. For me nothing about God was safe; nothing was sure.

I didn't find security in my life in Christ until I understood that as a believer, I'm sealed by the Holy Spirit. I credit my understanding of this important truth to a sermon John Piper preached the same year I walked the aisle of my church as a seven-year-old girl who was just trying to get it right. I wouldn't hear this sermon until years later, but it rocked me to my core, answered numerous questions, and opened my eyes to my security in Christ through the sealing of the Holy Spirit.

Sealed

sphragiz

1) to set a seal upon, mark with a seal, to seal

1a) for security: from Satan[6]

Piper says . . .

What does it mean that believers have been *sealed by the Holy Spirit* (v. 13)? The word is used at least three different ways in the New Testament.

1. In Matthew 27:66, the tomb of Jesus was secured by *sealing* it and putting guards around it. In Revelation 20:3 God throws Satan into a pit and *seals* it over so he can't escape. So one meaning is locking something up, closing it in.

2. Another is found in Romans 4:11 where Abraham's circumcision is called the sign and *seal* of the righteousness he had by faith. And in 1 Corinthians 9:2 Paul says that his converts are the *seal* of his apostleship. So a second meaning of sealing is giving a sign of authenticity.

3. A third meaning is found in Revelation 7:3 where the *seal* of God is put on the forehead of God's servants to protect them from the wrath coming upon the world.

So what did Paul mean in Ephesians 1:13 when he said that believers are sealed with the Holy Spirit? No matter which of these meanings you use the basic truth is the same.

1. If the Spirit *seals shut*, the point must be that he seals in faith and seals out unbelief and apostasy.

2. If the Spirit seals us as a *sign of authenticity*, then he is that sign and it is the Spirit's work in our life which is God's trademark. Our eternal sonship is real and authentic if we have the Spirit. He is the sign of divine reality in our lives.

3. Or if the Spirit *marks us with God's seal*, he protects us from evil forces which won't dare to enter a person bearing the mark of God's own possession.

However you come at this message contained in this word "sealed," it is a message of safety and security in God's love and power. God sends the Holy Spirit as a preserving seal to lock in our faith, as an authenticating seal to validate our sonship, and as a protecting seal to keep out destructive forces. The point is that God wants us to feel secure and safe in his love and power.[7]

I am guaranteed an inheritance (Ephesians 1:14).

_____

_____

_____

_____

This being "in Christ" through a relationship with the triune God is what the soul ultimately longs for. This place, within the realm of His protection and blessing, is the end destination of our

pursuit of in-ness, for "we live in God; we move in God; we exist in God" (Acts 17:28).

In Christ we have been blessed beyond measure. His shed blood was payment for our sin debt, a debt that we couldn't pay. His self-less sacrifice opened the door for us to receive the limitless grace and forgiveness God desired to rain down upon us. Jesus Christ delivered us from the chains of the enemy, setting us free to bring Him honor and glory through our lives.

Paul used his words to praise and applaud God for what He'd done in the lives of believers through Christ. We, too, are to praise God for every blessing that He's bestowed upon us. That's our mission individually and corporately; it's our way of honoring and glorifying Him.

Read Ephesians 1:3–14 again, this time keeping in mind these verses are a hymn of praise. Consider underlining the closing phrase of each stanza of praise, "to the praise of His glory" (NKJV), as you read. Each of these stanzas beautifully sums up our life mission.

In Christ . . . It's the only "in" worth being a part of. For it's in Him that we find freedom, purpose, and acceptance. In Christ, the grip of the enemy is severed and salvation is freely given. And it's to the praise of His glory that we live and breathe and work together to make Him known.

 e. (embrace)

Spend the rest of today praising God for blessing you, choosing you, predestining you to adoption, accepting you, redeeming you, forgiving you, enlightening you to spiritual things, sealing you with the Holy Spirit of promise, and guaranteeing you an inheritance in Christ. Praise God for making you one in Him through His beloved Son.

Write a praise poem or song to God, applauding His greatness.

_____

_____

_____

_____

_____

_____

_____

_____

d.i.v.e. into LESSON THREE

d. (define.)

i. (investigate.)

v. (visualize.)

e. (embrace.)

Meaning Behind the Message

Ephesians 1:15-23

 <u>Before you begin</u> your time of study and learning, spend a few moments in prayer asking God to give you an open heart and mind to learn new truths from His Word.

 ### v. (visualize)

Take a snapshot of Ephesians 1 by reading through the chapter at least three times, reminding yourself of the big picture. Review your WOW from chapter 1. Don't forget to add to your outline/paraphrase.

In this lesson we're going to zoom in on Ephesians 1:15–23. As you read these verses again, begin to d.i.v.e. below the surface.

FAITH AND LOVE

Read Ephesians 1:15–16.

In the first fourteen verses of Ephesians 1, Paul talks of the believer's unity in Christ and the blessings that are brought about by being made one in Him. In the latter part of this chapter, he shifts his thoughts in order to help us better understand what those blessings mean.

There are two specific phrases in verse 15 that we're going to d.i.v.e. into:

- ❥ faith in the Lord Jesus
- ❥ love for all God's people

Faith in the Lord Jesus and love for all God's people are two dimensions of the spiritual life that are inseparable. True faith in God will yield true love for others.

d. (define)

Based on your understanding right now of the word *faith*, define it in the space that follows. Don't look ahead for an answer, and don't rack your brain trying to come up with one. Just write down what you believe faith to be. If you don't have any idea, that's okay! If you can't seem to put your thoughts into words, try drawing a picture of "faith" in the margin.

_____

_____

_____

Faith is a complete trust and allegiance to something or someone. It's a belief or trust in. Paul had heard of the believers' faith in the Lord Jesus, and he gave thanks for it.

When I read verses like Ephesians 1:15–16, I always begin questioning. I don't question God's Word, but my mind goes deeper into thought. And questions run through my crazy brain, like these . . .

- ❥ Was their faith in the Lord Jesus enough to make them one in Christ?

♥ Is *my* faith or belief in Jesus enough to make *me* one in Christ?

I was always taught that if you "just believe in Jesus" you'll be saved, made right with God, miss out on hell, and gain entrance into heaven. And, mind you, Scripture does teach us that if we believe in our heart that God raised Jesus from the dead, we'll be saved. But, there's always the thought, *But that seems far too easy for me.* Maybe there is for you too. It just seems to me that there's a little more than just belief involved in this whole "being saved" experience.

Read James 2:19 from the New King James Version. Fill in the blanks.

You _____ that there is one God. You do well.

Even the demons _____—and tremble!

d. (define)

The word *faith* in Ephesians 1:15 and the word *believe* in James 2:19 are translations of the same Greek word: *pistis,* which comes from the Greek root word *peithō.*

James 2:19

Believe (pisteuō)
From *pistis;* to *have faith* (in, upon, or with respect to, a person or thing), that is, *credit;* by implication to *entrust:* —believe (-r), commit (to trust), put in trust with.

Ephesians 1:15

Faith (pistis)
From *peithō; persuasion,* that is, *credence;* moral *conviction,* assurance, belief, believe, faith, fidelity.

Peithō

(A primary verb)
to agree, assure, believe, have confidence, be (wax) content, make friend, obey, persuade, trust, yield.

If asked, "Do you believe in Jesus?" your answer would most likely be "Yes!" But does answering, "Yes, I believe in Jesus," position one within the realm of God's safekeeping? Is belief in Jesus all it takes to make a person one in Christ? Scripture tells us that even the demons believe in Jesus and shudder at the mention of His name. Does the demon's belief give him the right to say he is one in Christ? Does his belief make him accepted in the Beloved or redeemed by the blood?

Let's dive deeper into this question: What makes the belief of the demons different from the belief of the redeemed sinner?

Read Romans 10:5–10.

Here's where the belief of these two parties differs: belief on the part of the sinner is followed by **repentance**, a turning away from sin toward God; **confession**, agreeing with God that one has done wrong against Him; and finally, an **acknowledgment** of and **yielding** to Him as Lord and Savior.

Christ being Lord over the believer's life means He is the Master, possessing ultimate power and authority. Christ positioned as Lord places us as His slaves. When we submit to His lordship, we're relinquishing all control, surrendering completely to Him. This Master-servant relationship isn't one of bondage and impoverishment, but of freedom and riches from heaven.

Read Romans 6:19–22 from The Voice. Compare the "slaves to corrupt and lawless living" to the "slaves to right and reconciled" living.

_____

_____

_____

With Jesus Christ as the sovereign Lord of our lives, you and I are slaves to God, a position that leads to holiness and eternal life.

Let's revisit the question, Is belief enough to make a person one in Christ? Just with these few verses, I think we can see that for a person to be made one in Christ, belief must be accompanied by *repentance, confession*, and *surrender* of one's life. Now, I want you to understand something: none of us are perfect after salvation. But for the heart that's experienced Jesus-transformation on the inside, there will be a moving toward deeper, holy living.

LOVE FOR ALL GOD'S PEOPLE

Christ's lordship is evidenced by the fruit we bear, the fruit of our "love for all God's people." Paul commends these believers for their display of love for one another and encourages them to continue loving one another with the love of Christ that reigns in their hearts.

A Christian is not to be a respecter of persons. God loves sacrificially and selflessly, and we're to mirror this love. We're to love freely out of the abundant love that God bestowed upon us. Genuine love for others does "not love with word or with tongue, but in deed and truth" (1 John 3:18 NASB). Love is action. It's not a feeling or emotion, and it isn't motivated by what it can gain but by what it can give.

If one claims to love God, then love for his brother must be evident. The two go hand in hand.

Read 1 John 3:16–18 in the New King James Version. Fill in the blanks.

By this we know _____, because He laid down His life for us. And we also ought to lay down our lives for the brethren. But whoever has this world's goods, and sees his brother in need, and shuts up his heart from him, how does the_____ of God abide in him? My little children, let us not_____ in word or in tongue, but in _____ and in _____.

What about loving people who have wronged us or hurt us greatly? Does God expect us to love *those* individuals? How often I've wished the answer to be a big fat "NO!" but the reality is a resounding "YES!" God does expect us to love those who've wounded us. Is it easy? No. Not at all. Loving people who've abandoned us, lied to us, cheated on us, broken our hearts, taken from us, rejected us, or _____ is extremely difficult.

When it comes to loving people who've hurt me, my tendency is to deem them unlovable and unforgivable, shut them out of my life completely, and hold a grudge against them from now until forever. For years that's exactly how I treated those who'd hurt me; and I felt completely justified in doing so because in my mind they didn't deserve my love or forgiveness.

But I've learned some very important things about loving and forgiving "unlovables."

I am an unlovable myself. I've hurt others time and time again. I've done my share of inflicting wounds on those closest to me. I've rejected people I didn't feel were good enough for me. I've lied, cheated, stolen. Very unlovable indeed. I've wronged people, but I've also wronged God. I've sinned against Him in unimaginable ways while claiming to be "a child of God." I've rejected Him time and time again. I've lied to Him, cursed Him, and screamed at the top of my lungs, "I HATE YOU!" On my own, I'll always be undeserving of God's love and forgiveness. But His grace has been greater than all my sins, and His forgiveness has been showered down upon me. I've learned to look through God's eyes at those I've deemed unlovable and unforgivable and see them as He sees them: precious. If God can love me beyond my flaws and forgive me time and time again, then I can extend that same grace to those who've hurt me. And I pray that those I've hurt are able to extend that grace to me.

In my own strength I cannot love those who've hurt me. In Christ is the only place where the power to love and forgive can flow from me. When I allow Him to be completely in control of my life, my selfish desires to seek revenge and hold grudges vanish. When I've humbled myself to Christ's leading, I'm able to move past the hurt, knowing He'll use it for His good. Loving and forgiving aren't easy, but they're possible when we see others as God sees them and walk in His power.

Allowing God to reign in one's life as Lord and Master means humbly submitting to His instruction and leading. And just as peace flows from grace, so does love flow from a true faith in Jesus Christ.

 e. (embrace)

Who is Lord of your life? Is Christ in control or are you? How are you doing loving and forgiving those "unlovables" in your life?

Spend time in prayer right now. Admit to God those areas over which you're struggling to let Him have control. Ask Him to help you let go and trust His leading. Share with God your pain from being hurt by others. Ask Him to give you the power to love and forgive those who've wronged you. Thank God for loving and forgiving you for the times you've sinned against Him. And as you spend time talking with God, know that He may lead you to go to others and seek forgiveness for the wrongs you've done against them. Friend, obey His leading. If you'd rather pray "on paper," write out your prayer here.

_____

_____

_____

_____

_____

_____

STOP LOOKING! IT'S ALREADY YOURS!

Read Ephesians 1:17–23.

It was just a blue ink pen, but I was in a panic. Like a madwoman, I was scouring my desk for the missing pen, which was supposed to be paired with the cap I held in my hand. Yes, I'm an office supply junkie, a lover of Post-it notes, colored pens, and cutesy binder clips, and when I lose my pens, the planets no longer align as they should.

One by one I asked everyone in my department if they'd seen my pen. "Are you sure?" I begged, showing them the cap in hopes it would jog their memories, but no one had seen it.

I searched the restroom, break room, and warehouse. No pen. Defeated, I plopped down in my chair and let out a deep sigh. My coworker peeked her head around our cubicle wall. "Any luck?"

"Nope, it's gone."

As I began to run my fingers through my hair to put it up in a ponytail, I felt a foreign object over my right ear. I let out a scream, "My pen!"

Forty-five minutes of frantic searching for something I'd never lost.

Sadly, many Christians find themselves in the same situation, frantically searching for something without realizing it's already in their possession.

It was Paul's desire in writing this letter for believers to know and understand all they possess in Christ—all that already belongs to them. He prayed not for an increase in material possessions for these believers, but for their lives to be deepened spiritually. He wanted them to experience an enlightenment regarding the riches of God's grace and the spiritual blessings that accompany it.

🖋 Who is the "Spirit of wisdom and revelation" (NKJV)?

_____

Read Isaiah 11:2; John 14:25–26; and John 16:12–14. You and I can't understand the things of God apart from the Holy Spirit opening our minds and hearts. The Holy Spirit unearths for us truths from the Word, gives wisdom and knowledge to know how to apply those truths, and empowers us to live them out.

🖋 **Read Ephesians 1:18.** For what purpose does this "enlightenment" come?

_____

_____

_____

In the New King James Version, Paul prays that "the eyes of your understanding [be] enlightened" (v. 18). The NIV reads, "That the eyes of your heart may be enlightened." How can the eyes of your understanding or the eyes of your heart be "enlightened"? It sounds a little odd, doesn't it?

Two things will help us better understand what Paul is talking about here:

1. Look at the Greek. *Understanding,* according to Thayer's Greek Definitions, means "the mind as a faculty of understanding, feeling, desiring; understanding; mind, i.e. spirit, way of thinking and feeling; thoughts, either good or bad."[1]

2. Think of the heart of man as being his emotional core. Often in Scripture, the "heart" also speaks to man's inner being, which includes not only his emotions, but also the mind and the will. It's the center of knowledge, understanding, thinking, and wisdom.

The inner person has spiritual senses that parallel the physical senses. The inner man, the emotions, the mind, and the will become alive when we're made one in Christ.

Read 1 Corinthians 2:9–13. What does Paul say about the Spirit of God?

_____

_____

_____

Read Ephesians 1:17–23 in the NKJV again; then break down these verses and list the four prayers Paul prayed for his brothers and sisters in Christ.

1._____

2._____

3._____

4._____

How did you do? Here are the four things Paul prayed believers would do:

1. Know God: "revelation in the knowledge of Him" (v. 17 NKJV).

Paul had experienced firsthand what it meant to have a personal, intimate relationship with God. He'd met God through the person of Jesus Christ and was changed completely from the inside out. He knew God as Savior, Friend, Father, Guide, Protector, Provider, and Lord.

Further, the Holy Spirit had opened Paul's mind to understand the things and ways of God. It was the Holy Spirit who revealed the divine truth of God's plan for Paul's life. And it was the Holy Spirit who empowered Paul to fulfill the work God had called him to do.

2. Know God's calling: "that you may know what is the hope of His calling" (v. 18 NKJV).

A *calling* is an invitation to join another in a work. It's God's good pleasure and perfect will to call believers to join Him in making His name known throughout the land. Remember: God calls us to Himself by grace alone. Nothing we've ever done or will do merits our receiving this invitation from God. It's His sovereign choice whom He'll invite into His royal family. God's calling is filled with hope, steering us forward to the day Jesus Christ will return for His bride, the church.

Without Christ we have no hope. But, in Christ Jesus we have a "living hope" (1 Peter 1:3) that gives us the strength we need to live life with passion and purpose.

3. Know God's abundant riches: "what are the riches of the glory of His inheritance in the saints" (v. 18 NKJV).

In Ephesians 1:11 we read, "In Him also we have obtained an inheritance" (NKJV)—that inheritance being salvation, eternal life, Jesus, and all that belongs to Him. Here in verse 18 of Ephesians 1, Paul speaks to the fact that we are an inheritance to God. You and I are part of God's great wealth. He counts us as treasures! We're part of the "glory of His grace" that will bring Him praise upon His return.

Read what Warren W. Wiersbe says in relation to our being an inheritance to God:

> God deals with us on the basis of our future, not on our past. He said to cowardly Gideon, "The LORD is with thee, thou mighty man of valor" (Judges 6:12). Jesus said to Andrew's brother, "Thou art Simon . . . thou shalt be called Cephas [a stone]" (John 1:42).
>
> Gideon did become a mighty man of valor, and Simon did become Peter, a rock. We Christians live in the future tense, our lives controlled by what we shall be when Christ returns. Because we are God's inheritance, we live to please and glorify Him.[2]

"God deals with us on the basis of our future, not on our past." What a beautiful promise that God sees me for what He can make me and not the person I was in my sinful past! I pray we cling to this beautiful promise that we're His inheritance and live lives that bring Him honor and glory.

4. Know God's magnificent power: "and what is the surpassing greatness of His **power** toward us who believe. These are in accordance with the **working** of the **strength** of His **might** which He brought about in Christ, when He raised Him from the dead and seated Him at His right hand in the heavenly places, far above all rule and authority and power and dominion, and every name that is named, not only in this age but also in the one to come. And He put all things in subjection under His feet, and gave Him as head over all things to the church, which is His body, the fullness of Him who fills all in all" (vv. 19–23 NASB; emphasis added).

God displayed to us His great love by making us a part of His inheritance through Christ's shed blood on the cross. In promising us a hope-filled calling, He invited us to join Him in His working here on earth sharing with others a hope for today and a hope for the future offered only by God. Paul challenges believers to live out their callings fueled by the power of God actively working in them.

But just as I frantically searched for a blue ink pen that was already in my possession, far too often we fail to realize that God's power already belongs to us. At the moment of salvation, we're filled to the full with the power of the Holy Spirit. And this is the very same supernatural power, working, strength, and might with which God worked in Christ when He raised Him from the dead and seated Him at His right hand in the heavenly places. It's like power on steroids, times a gazillion!

Why do you think Paul used so many words to describe God's power? What do you think is the message he was trying to convey?

_____

_____

_____

_____

Read Ephesians 1:22–23. Who is the head over all things?

_____

Who makes up "His body"?

_____

In verse 23, the idea of the church being *a body* is introduced to us for the first time. Paul wrote much about the church—its purpose, mission, and unity—in this particular letter. We'll talk more about that in later chapters. Right now, we need to understand this very important fact: Christ is head over all things for the benefit of His body, the church. Paul's use of this picture of the body is multifaceted in purpose: (1) Christ being the head shows us that He is Lord; (2) the church as the body shows we're unified, working together under His leadership and direction; and (3) it further supports Paul's teaching that believers are "in Christ"—that we live and move and exist in Him (Acts 17:28).

 e. (embrace)

Paul desired for all believers to understand the greatness of God's power in their lives, a power available to us through a living and active faith. Will you today experience God's power unleashed in your life, enabling you to understand His riches, His calling, and His person?

Operation Peace

EPHESIANS TWO

d.i.v.e. into LESSON ONE

d. (define)

i. (investigate)

v. (visualize)

e. (embrace)

Life After Death

Ephesians 2:1-10

 Before you begin your time of study and learning, spend a few moments in prayer asking God to give you an open heart and mind to learn new truths from His Word.

 ## v. (visualize)

Take a snapshot of Ephesians 2 by reading through the chapter at least three times so you understand the big picture. As you're reading make note of any verse(s) that tugs at your heart; this may be the WOW God wants you to embrace from chapter 2. Begin to develop your own outline/paraphrase.

In this lesson we're going to zoom in on Ephesians 2:1–10. As you read these verses again, begin to d.i.v.e. below the surface.

THE DARKNESS OF DEATH

Read Ephesians 2:1–3.

In my junior year of college, I was required to take a class that involved a chaplaincy internship at the Baptist Hospital in Pensacola, Florida. Late one night while I was asleep in my dorm, a call came in. "There's been a death on Oncology. We have to go now," the chaplain mentor said as she ran past my room.

The night was dark and crazy quiet as mist and fog blanketed the parking lot. We hurried through the ER entrance and made a beeline for the elevator. As the elevator doors closed, my chaplain mentor got right in my face, grabbed both my shoulders, and said, "You're taking the lead on this call because you need to grow up. You've got a lot to learn about life." I had no time to protest because the elevator bell rang, the doors slid open, and it was time to face death.

Screams, wailing, curse words. *Oh my gosh! Have we just entered the Twilight Zone?* I stood frozen in *oh-heck-no-I-didn't-sign-up-for-this.* My mentor pushed me forward into the middle of utter chaos, and because I was wearing a "Chaplain" badge, a nurse took me by the arm, quickly walked me down the hall, and stopped outside a closed door room.

More screaming and wailing, along with huffing, puffing, and *stomping.* "We can't get her to stop. She's been in there since he died," the nurse said. "I sure hope you can help."

And away she went.

I twisted the doorknob and cautiously pushed open the door. She was on top of him. *Oh no she's not!* That sister was on top of her dead brother, shaking him, screaming, and begging him to wake up. *What in the world?*

She heard the door creak and turned back to look. "Help me!" she yelled. "He won't wake up. He has to wake up!"

"Um, ma'am, I'm sorry, but he's not going to wake up. He's dead," I whispered, completely horrified.

She was crying uncontrollably. Her nose was pouring snot. She would shake him, and then beat his chest. *That was the stomping. This is crazy!*

"He has to wake up. He can't be dead," she kept saying, over and over again.

But he was dead. His body was without life. He wasn't breathing, and there was no amount of shaking or beating, screaming, or begging that was going to bring this man back to life.

Minutes passed. Exhausted, the sister collapsed on top of her brother, realizing he was indeed gone from this life. She lay there motionless, having fought the battle of her life. Death had defeated her.

Dead and defeated. It was the reality of my life before Jesus. But my death wasn't physical; it was a death of spiritual proportions. I had no control over it and no more ability to revive myself than that sister had to revive her dead brother. It didn't matter how many church services I attended, Bible studies I signed up for, Compassion International children I sponsored, or Christian books I read, without Jesus the truth of my spiritual position was one of death.

> **All** have sinned, and **all** their futile attempts to reach God in His glory fail.
> –Romans 3:23 (bold emphasis added)

In fact, Paul says in Ephesians 2:1, "dead" is the reality of all our lives without Christ, and there's nothing any of us can do about it. Yes, we were created to be in *Christ*, but dead in *trespasses and sins* is where we find ourselves because of the sin nature passed down to us by Adam.

🖋 **Leave Ephesians for a few minutes and read the following verses.** Record what they say about our sin nature: Genesis 5:3; Psalm 51:5; Romans 5:12

_____

_____

_____

_____

_____

d. (define)

🖋 Use a *Strong's Concordance* to define *trespasses* and *sins* as found in Ephesians 2:1 (NKJV).

Trespasses

_____

_____

_____

Sins

_____

_____

_____

Let's sum it up . . . both trespasses and sins

● represent acts done against God and a failure to follow Him.

● cause us to be separated from the almighty God.

● place us in a position of needing a Savior.

🖋 **Read Ephesians 2:1–3** again. Pull these verses apart, listing the characteristics of one who is dead in trespasses and sins. Take some time to read and examine the cross-references that are given in your Bible to gain better clarity and explanation of these characteristics and their origin.

Verse 1	Verse 2	Verse 3
	John 1:9; 2 Corinthians 10:4-5; Colossians 1:21; John 12:31; Ephesians 6:12	1 Peter 4:3; Galatians 5:16; Psalm 51:5
Ephesians 4:18		

We'll d.i.v.e. deeper into the profile of our enemy later in the study, but I don't want us to bypass this mention of him in these few verses, because it's here that Paul reminds us of the one who holds the dead man captive.

🖋 Throughout Scripture, specifically the New Testament, the enemy, Satan, is given different names or titles. **Read the following verses** and list the names that are mentioned for him: John 12:31; 14:30; 16:11; 2 Corinthians 4:4; Ephesians 2:2; 1 John 5:19.

_____

_____

_____

In looking at our enemy and the power he has, we must understand and remember a few important truths:

1. Satan doesn't have complete rule or control over the world. God is sovereign. In His infinite wisdom, He has simply allowed Satan, within allotted boundaries, to roam this earth, "*hoping for the chance* to devour someone" (1 Peter 5:8).

2. Satan has control only over the spiritually dead. Those who are dead are caught in the "devil's snare" (2 Timothy 2:26), are "in the grips of the evil one" (1 John 5:19), and are being controlled by Satan (Ephesians 2:2). But those who've said yes to following Jesus—who've positionally moved from death to life—are no longer under his control (Colossians 1:13).

UNDER THE INFLUENCE OF THE HOLY SPIRIT

In Ephesians 2:3 Paul says, "We were all guilty of falling headlong for the persuasive passions of this world; we all have had our fill of indulging the flesh and mind."

 i. (investigate)

Read Galatians 5:19–21.

 What are the heinous acts of the flesh?

_____

_____

_____

_____

How can we fight against the cravings to commit those acts? Fill in the blanks.

Here's my instruction: walk in the _____, and let the _____ bring order to your life. If you do, you will never give in to your _____.

—Galatians 5:16

Walking in the Spirit will give us victory over the flesh by weakening its power. If we d.i.v.e. below the surface meaning of this phrase "walk in the Spirit," we'll find the word *walk* in the original Greek language is a present imperative, which simply means "keep on walking." So walking in the Spirit is a continual process, a habitual lifestyle; it's a day-by-day, moment-by-moment aligning of ourselves with Him, placing our feet in His footprints. If He steps to the right, we step to the right; if He steps to the left, we follow suit. If the Spirit presses on straight ahead, then we, too, forward march.

In walking in the power of the Holy Spirit and experiencing victory over the cravings, or, as many versions put it, lusts of the flesh, I've come to realize that there are four things I *must* do daily:

1. I must surrender control by admitting my need for God. As much as I try to handle things on my own, I can't do it all. I need God. Every day. All day. I'm a mess waiting to happen without Him! (See Luke 22:42.)

2. I must get in the Word and d.i.v.e. deep for His truth. I know that sounds cliché, but if I don't get into God's Word daily and feed on the richness there, I'll feed on something else: TV, Facebook, Twitter, relationships, etc. I have to open wide my mouth, heart, mind, and soul, and let the words of Jesus fill me full. (See Psalm 81:10.)

3. I must find community. I'm a loner by nature, yet internally I scream for a community of people to walk beside. Although it's

very hard, I purposefully put myself out there in order to be encouraged and challenged by others in the body of Christ. (See Ephesians 4:15–16.)

4. I must exercise myself toward godliness. To walk in the Spirit, I must let go of my selfish will and surrender completely to God's will, plan, and way. I must confess sin quickly, trust God to do what's best, and be obedient in every aspect of my life. (See 1 Timothy 4:7–8.)

 e. (embrace)

Are you walking in the Spirit so as not to give in to your selfish and sinful cravings? Does your life reflect full submission to the Spirit's leading? If not, what steps do you need to take to begin walking in the Spirit?

_____

_____

_____

THE WRATH OF GOD

As we head back to Ephesians 2:3, I want to give you a pep talk before we get there. We've got to tackle something we usually steer clear of because, quite frankly, it's uncomfortable and a little unnerving. But if we're to rightly investigate the words Paul has shared and grasp the reality of the place in which the dead man lives, it's a conversation we must have. So, come a little closer and let's d.i.v.e. in.

Read Ephesians 2:3, focusing on the last sentence.

We were all guilty of falling headlong for the persuasive passions of this world; we all have had our fill of indulging the flesh and mind, obeying impulses to follow perverse thoughts motivated by dark powers. As a result, our natural inclinations led us to be children of wrath, just like the rest of humankind.

We're born with a sin nature; in simple terms this means we have a natural bent to do the exact opposite of what God's Word teaches, leaving Him out of our lives. We're guilty of doing our own thing, giving in to our wants and desires, thinking only about ourselves, clearly not living under the influence of the Holy Spirit, but remaining dead in trespasses and sins. And "as a result, our natural inclinations led us to be" objects of the wrath of God.

You might be asking yourself, "Does the wrath of God mean He gets angry?" Here's where things get uncomfortable for me because I don't want to think of God being angry with me. I mean, goodness gracious! The all-powerful God of the universe, *angry* with me? The thought freaks me out.

So it helps for me to put the reality of being an object of God's wrath in perspective. We must remember: not only is God powerful and the ruler of the universe; He's our Daddy. And like any loving parent, He won't tolerate disobedience, not because He's just waiting to give us a holy spanking but because He desires the best for us; He wants us to live holy and righteous lives. Our heavenly Father's wrath is an extension of His deep love.

But in our human frailty, we can't bear the weight of God's wrath; it would blow us to smithereens. Jesus, God in flesh, was the only person who could take on God's wrath. And because of God's great love and desire to be in intimate relationship with us, moving

us from the shallows to the deep, He willingly gave His Son over to receive, in our place, the brunt of His wrath.

Yes, God gets angry. Yes, as those dead in trespasses and sins, we're objects of His anger. But as our loving Father, He directed His wrath against us to His Son who, as our atoning sacrifice, saved us from God's wrath.

Take a few minutes to **read and investigate the following verses**. What do they teach about Jesus becoming the object of God's wrath in our place? John 3:36; Romans 3:23–25; 5:9–10; Hebrews 2:17; 1 John 2:2; 4:10

_____

_____

_____

_____

_____

Let's stop for a minute and quickly recap what we just learned:

- Without Christ all of humanity is dead in trespasses and sins. This isn't a physical death but a spiritual one that separates us from God. It's a death over which we have no control, leaving us defeated and incapable of awakening from the darkness.

- As a spiritually dead person, one's life is lived according to the pattern of the world—a world ruled by Satan. It's a life that finds one indulging his flesh and mind.

- Every person, because of his sinful nature, is an object of God's wrath. "Condemnation is already the reality for everyone who refuses to believe because they reject the name of the only Son of God." (John 3:18).

Seems pretty grim, huh? If we were to stop reading at Ephesians 2:3, close our Bibles and put them away, our lives would seem to be without hope. Thankfully though, there is hope, and "dead in trespasses and sins" (v. 1 NKJV) doesn't have to be the end. Why? Because we have a God who loves us dearly and desires to have a deeply intimate relationship with us.

 Read Ephesians 2:4–10. What are the first two words of Ephesians 2:4?

But God . . .

But God, who is rich in mercy, loved a sinful people with a love so amazing we no longer have to "live dead" because of our trespasses and sins.

But God, who overflows with an undeserved kindness toward those He chose in Him before the foundation of the world, makes us alive in Christ.

But God, who lavished His grace on a people who had absolutely nothing to offer Him, raised us up to new life in Christ.

SHOWTIME

Imagine with me for a moment we're in an arena full of people who've gathered for an event. The house lights have gone black and a spotlight shines on the person standing center stage. We find ourselves waiting backstage to be introduced as the keynote speakers for the event. Our hearts pound, our knees quiver, our mouths are dry, and our bodies go numb. I've decided to take one for the team and be the first to stand in the midst of this crowd of onlookers. I hear my name called.

"Jenifer Jernigan . . ." *Echo. Echo. Echo.*

The words are muffled, and I think I might vomit. The announcer continues, but I only hear bits and pieces of what's being said . . .

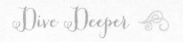

"She has been a great disappointment to her family. She's lived much of her life in the shallows of religion trying to live up to the expectations of those around her. She is a rule-following, people-pleasing, fear-walking, guilt-ridden addict, who fails more than she succeeds. Her husband wanted to divorce her and her kids thought she was an alligator because she was always snappy and mean. Shame and guilt have been her best friends much of her life. And Reject could be her middle name."

Yep, I'm sure I'll vomit! But then my ears tune in completely to the words that now fill the arena . . .

"But God"

". . . but God, who is rich in mercy, scooped this rule-following, people-pleasing, fear-walking, guilt-ridden addict up into His strong hands and transformed her from the inside out through the healing power of the Word, leading her from ritualistic religion to deep faith in Him. Shame and guilt have been kicked to the curb, and her new best friends are grace and forgiveness. She's learning to live free and glorify God in all she does. Ladies and gentlemen . . ."

But God, who is rich in mercy because of His great love for me . . . He is the only One who can step into the muck and mire of my mess and pull me from the grip of the enemy. He is the only One who can erase the past and lead me into the beautiful future He planned just for me.

 e. (embrace)

Now it's your turn to take center stage, but let's skip over what might have been said and head straight to your "but God" introduction.

What would be said about you? Write it here, and praise God for
His rich mercy toward you.

_____

_____

_____

_____

_____

_____

_____

YOU RAISE ME UP

Read Ephesians 2:6–7. What do you think it means for a believer
to be raised up and seated with Christ in the heavenly realms?

_____

_____

_____

Just as Christ was raised physically from the dead, believers are
raised up from a "dead" life to a new, living, breathing-in, breathing-
out life in Christ. This new life grants us the honor of being seated
with Christ in His heavenly home. Think of it as a permanent
change of address:

7 Golden Street Way

New Jerusalem, Heaven 77777

"For all eternity," in our forever heavenly home, God will show "the
incredible riches of His grace and kindness that He freely gives to
us by uniting us with Jesus the Anointed" (v. 7). Use your Bible's

cross-references to d.i.v.e. deeper into the incredible riches of God's grace toward us and how we'll honor and thank Him for lavishing this grace upon our sin-sick hearts. I'll help you get started—d.i.v.e. into:

Revelation 7:10–12

_____

_____

_____

_____

When I stood beside that sister who'd just lost her brother, watching her beat his chest, shake his shoulders, and scream at the top of her lungs to try to revive him, I knew nothing would bring that man back to life. She was powerless over his death. And if we step back and look at the reality of our spiritual death, we'll see that we, too, are powerless. There's absolutely nothing we can do to save ourselves from spiritual death.

Read Ephesians 2:8. How is a person who is dead in trespasses and sins saved?

_____

_____

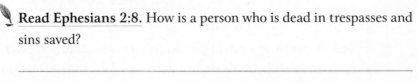

God gifts us with grace and gives us the faith
to trust in Him for salvation. It's only through
the avenue of faith that salvation comes.

Read the following verses. What do they say about grace, faith, and salvation?

Galatians 2:16

_____

_____

1 Peter 1:5

_____

_____

Philippians 1:29

_____

_____

Acts 3:16

_____

_____

d.i.v.e. DEEPER . . . PURPOSEFUL FAITH

Read Ephesians 2:8 paired with verse 9. Is a person saved because of his own efforts, or, as the New King James calls it, his "works"? Why or why not?

_____

_____

_____

_____

_____

Our works or "good deeds" have nothing to with our salvation. Salvation is God's gift to those He predestined to obtain His inheritance. Good works don't produce salvation, but our salvation will produce good works. (Ephesians 1:5, 11)

Fill in the blank.

"By this My Father is glorified, that you _____ much fruit; so you will be My disciples."

—John 15:8 (NKJV)

Let's zoom out of Ephesians for a few minutes and visit with James as we d.i.v.e deeper into purposeful faith. The waters are going to get pretty deep here, but don't swim away! Swim with me into the current of truth. Consider the following verses:

James 2:17: Without actions, *faith is useless. By itself,* it's *as good as* dead.

James 2:20: Faith has to show itself through works performed in faith.

James 2:26: Removing action from faith is like removing breath from a body. All you have left is a corpse.

What do you think Scripture means when it says faith without works is *"as good as* dead" and *"useless"*?

_____

_____

When it comes to understanding these three verses, there are two possibilities to consider:

One: Faith without works is not enough. (A person's works produce his or her salvation.)

Two: Faith without works is not "living" (active) faith.

Which of these two thoughts do you think is correct when James says that faith without works is dead/useless? Share your thoughts in the space that follows.

_____

_____

_____

Not sure? Let me help:

Read James 2:14 from the New Living Translation:

What good is it, dear brothers and sisters, if you say you have faith but don't show it by your actions? Can that kind of faith save anyone?

Can "that kind of faith [a faith not shown by its actions] save anyone?" Why or why not?

_____

_____

_____

_____

_____

> "Faith without works is dead also" (James 2:26 NKJV).

Read James 2:18 from the New King James Version:

But someone will say, "You have faith, and I have works." Show me your faith without your works, and I will show you my faith by my works."

How many "faiths" are mentioned here? What are they?

_____

_____

Remember that "living" faith is faith that is responding to God's gift of salvation.

Not only is this faith "living" and responding, but it is also purpose driven.

For what purpose does God give faith? **Read James 2:18–26.** What three examples are given here to show that "living" faith is given by God for the purpose of producing works?

_____

_____

_____

Read James 2:19. How do we know that the demons who "believe" do not have a faith that has been made living in Christ? Does the faith of a demon have a purpose?

_____

_____

In the beginning of our study, we talked about the importance of context and understanding the backstory. Before you jump into these last few verses in James, I encourage you to read more about Abraham's faith story in Genesis 22 and Rahab's faith story in Joshua 2; 6:22-25.

Read James 2:21–24. How do we know that Abraham had "living" faith? What purpose did his faith accomplish?

_____

_____

_____

_____

Read James 2:25. How do we know that Rahab had "living" faith? What purpose did her faith accomplish?

_____

_____

_____

_____

Faith without works is nothing more than mere head knowledge, shallow religion. But faith that produces good works in the life of its recipient evidences a heart that has been made alive in Christ, stepping from the shallow to the deep.

From James 2:14–26, we learn that living faith produces good works. In verse 14, James calls faith without works "that kind of faith" (NLT) to show us that there are two kinds of faith. This idea is reinforced in verse 18, where James clearly identifies two kinds of faith: one without works, and one with works.

The examples of the demons, Abraham, and Rahab in verses 19–26 make clear that living faith is given by God to accomplish His purposes. The demons do nothing with their "faith" but shudder. Abraham's faith accomplished a number of God's purposes, including being the father of God's chosen people. Another example of Abraham's living faith was his willingness to offer up his son when God asked him to, acting on his belief that God was sovereign over all things (Genesis 22:1–19). And finally, Rahab's faith allowed the Israelites' defeat of Canaan and established her in the genealogy of Jesus Christ (Matthew 1:5).

Let's head back to Ephesians 2:8–9 and revisit the question, Is a person saved because of his or her good works? The answer is a simple no. God gives us the faith to accept His gift of grace. Our "working" has nothing to do with whether or not God can save us; salvation is solely based on His grace and comes to us by way of faith.

Here's the bottom line . . .

Good works don't produce salvation;

salvation produces good works.

And it's those good works that God prepared beforehand for us to live out (Ephesians 2:10).

Let's wrap up this lesson by diving deeper into verse 10, looking at it in the New King James Version. I'm going to set the framework for you to do this exercise yourself. Take a deep breath and d.i.v.e. deeper in. Carefully go through this one verse. Make lists, define words, use cross references, ask investigative questions, visualize and paraphrase the text, and embrace God's challenge to you. Study the words God breathed through the apostle Paul. You can do it!

Here's the frame based on the New King James Version . . . you paint the picture.

For we are His workmanship, created in Christ Jesus for
good works, which God prepared beforehand that we
should walk in them. Ephesians 2:10, NKJV

d. (define)

workmanship
good works
*What words would you define?

 i. (investigate)

Who is God's workmanship?
Who are we created in?
What are we created for?
When did God prepare our good works?
How should we respond to those good works?
*What investigative questions would you ask of this verse?

 v. (visualize)

Remember how we visualize passages?
Use commas and punctuation marks as
your breaking points.

 e. (embrace)

What is Jesus challenging you to live more deeply?

d.i.v.e. into LESSON TWO

d. (define)

i. (investigate)

v. (visualize)

e. (embrace)

A Coming Together as One

Ephesians 2:11-13

 Before you begin your time of study and learning, spend a few moments in prayer, asking God to give you an open heart and mind to learn new truths from His Word.

 ### v. (visualize)

Take a snapshot of Ephesians 2 by reading through the chapter at least three times, reminding yourself of the big picture. Is there a WOW you're embracing and implanting in your heart? Take a few moments to review that verse(s). Don't forget to add to your outline/paraphrase.

In this lesson we're going to zoom in on Ephesians 2:11–13. As you read these verses again, begin to d.i.v.e. below the surface.

NEVER FORGET

A heads-up . . . In Ephesians 1–2:10, Paul's target audience has been believers in general. He's about to shift his attention from believers as a whole to a specific group of believers.

Paul begins the next part of his letter with the words, "So never forget . . ." The word *so* may seem insignificant, but that couldn't be farther from the truth. *So* is a conjunctive adverb. It joins two clauses and shows cause and effect.

In the previous verses Paul painted a picture of the dead man, the cause and stark reality of his death, and the beauty of his resurrection. As he wraps up Ephesians 2, he's going to paint two more pictures showing the effects of the dead man being made alive in Christ.

Read Ephesians 2:11–13.

"So" picture number 1.

Who is Paul addressing in these three verses and what is he asking them to do?

_____

_____

Paul's message to the Gentile believer . . . Never forget the past. They should never forget:

- that they were once dead in sin but are now alive in Christ.

- that they once lived under Satan's control and conducted themselves in the lust of the flesh but are now members of God's family, seated in the heavenly realms in Christ, and empowered by the Holy Spirit to live holy lives.

- that at one time they were objects of God's wrath—an anger so intense it could only be carried on Jesus' shoulders—but are now saved by grace.

- the richness of God's mercy and the immensity of His love.

- that, though once far away from God, through the shed blood of Jesus they have been brought so very near.

- who they once were, but live in who Jesus says they are.

I don't know about you, but I have a tendency to live in my past. To wallow in guilt, shame, and regret. To wish for do-overs and beg for second chances. To hang out in the land of shoulda, coulda, woulda and wonder "what might have been." I also have a tendency to live as a victim. To use past hurts and heartbreaks as reasons not to move forward but to stand frozen in fear, clenching my fists and gritting my teeth. To hold in my heart anger, resentment, and hatred toward those who've wounded me deeply. And to live life alone in my little corner of the world.

But I suspect if Paul and I were having coffee, he'd say to me, just as he did to the Gentile believers of his day, "Girl, never forget the past, but don't live there, because in Christ Jesus you've been hugged by a loving, caring, merciful God, who has removed you from that past and brought you into His glorious presence. Never forget who you were, how you lived, and what you lived in, but stand in the freedom of who Jesus now says you are."

Yes sir, Mr. Paul! Thank you for that pep talk!

Friend, listen: our pasts—the good, bad, and ugly—can haunt us like a nightmare, chaining us to hurts and regrets, but we have to wake up from that bad dream, break chains, dream new dreams, and live in the presence of Jesus! Remembering the past is good, but living there hinders us from moving forward. Remembering the past reminds us of what God has rescued us from. It enables us to relate to those who might be living through the same hurts and heartaches we've been healed of. It's important to never forget the past but vital that we live in Jesus.

e. (embrace)

I talk to myself quite often, and yes, I answer myself too. And because I have a love-hate relationship with my past, needing a constant reminder of who Jesus says I am, I often stand in front of my bathroom mirror and speak Jesus' truth into my heart. Maybe today you need to do the same. Stand in front of your bathroom mirror, look yourself in the eyes, and with your outside voice, speak these words . . .

> I am a child of God. I don't live in my past, nor am I defined by its happenings. I'm stepping forward from the shallows into deep, lasting faith in Jesus. I've been identified, defined, and refined by a merciful God who loved me when I hated Him and sent His only Son to bear upon His shoulders a punishment I could never endure. And I am cherished by a selfless Savior, who captured me and embraced me in my brokenness, loving me into His family, and a mighty Holy Spirit, who teaches and empowers and guides me to live out God's master plan for my life. I AM a child of God!

VISIBLE DISTINCTION

Read Ephesians 2:11 from the New King James Version and fill in the blanks.

Gentile believers were called _____.

Jewish believers were called _____.

Paul's audience of Gentile believers were familiar with the Old Testament and understood the nation of Israel had been set apart by God as His very own. For hundreds of years the Circumcision (Jews) had looked down upon the Uncircumcision (Gentiles), deeming them outcast and not good enough to be God's chosen.

Let's zoom out of Ephesians for a few minutes and investigate further how God marked His own.

Read Genesis 17:10–11. What was the sign that would separate God's chosen people from other nations?

_____

Investigate the following verses: Romans 8:28–29; Galatians 5:6; 6:15. What do they say about circumcision and uncircumcision?

_____

_____

_____

_____

_____

_____

Circumcision of the flesh set the nation of Israel apart from pagan nations, but it never marked their personal relationship with God. In the end, circumcision of the flesh doesn't matter; it's the

circumcision of the heart, the cutting off of one's sinfulness, that softens the heart and enables the individual to experience new life in Christ.

Read Romans 4:9–12. According to these verses, when was Abraham saved? Before or after he was circumcised?

_____

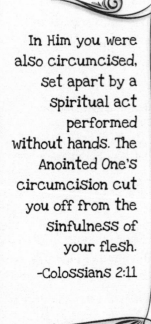

> In Him you were also circumcised, set apart by a spiritual act performed without hands. The Anointed One's circumcision cut you off from the sinfulness of your flesh.
>
> -Colossians 2:11

God's intended purpose for the physical sign of circumcision wasn't to put a wedge between His people and pagan nations. He intended for Israel to be an example, live holy, and point others to Him. Their being handpicked by God to display His greatness to the world was an honor, and with this honor came great responsibility. But instead of embracing their God-given birthright, Israel began to develop a sense of entitlement and a holier-than-thou attitude. Rituals and practices, although instituted by God, became the only acceptable standard by which to live. Rather than embracing and teaching and sharing their God with people different from themselves, Israel scoffed, turned their nose in the air, and hoarded God. Their spiritual lifestyle wasn't a reflection of what God had done for them or what He desired to do for all humankind; it was a reflection of selfishness and godless living.

SEPARATED FROM GOD

Let's focus back in on our text in Ephesians. **Read Ephesians 2:12;** then break this verse down and list the ways in which the Gentiles were separated from God and the nation of Israel.

1. _____

2._____

3._____

4._____

5._____

- The Gentile people had "no connection to the Anointed."

  This group of individuals had no link to God. They had no one leading them and no one guiding them. And without a Savior, they had no purpose.

- The Gentile people were "strangers, separated from God's people."

  The Gentiles didn't belong to the theocratic state of Israel. The Jews were governed by God; He was their King and Lord, and from Him came blessings and protection. The Gentile people were without this governing Leader, His blessings, and protection.

- The Gentile people were "aliens to the covenant they [Israel] had with God."

  God's covenants were personal promises He'd made to His people. These covenants would redeem, bless, prosper, save, and multiply the nation of Israel. Within the realm of these covenants, God promised land, a kingdom, and a King, the Messiah. While the Gentile nation is included in the "blanket blessing" of the covenant God made with Abraham (Genesis 12:1–3), He had made no personal covenants with them. Gentiles were, however, included in the new covenant God made that promised to all its recipients the blessings of salvation (Jeremiah 31:31–34; Hebrews 8:7–13; 10:11–18).

- The Gentile people "were hopelessly stranded."

  They were hopelessly stranded because they were without Christ, had no Ruler, and had not made "covenant" with God.

They lived their lives with no personal expectation that the Messiah to the Jews would be for them.

● The Gentile people were "without God in a *fractured* world."

It wasn't that the Gentile people were atheists; they did believe in god—many gods, in fact. But they didn't believe in Yahweh God. They were without Him, not because God had rejected them, but because they had rejected God.

From the outside looking into the inner circle of the Jewish nation, life looked hopeless for the Gentiles. But God had a plan—a plan that had been set in motion before the foundation of the world. Because, you see . . . our God makes no mistakes and does nothing without a purpose. His plan from the beginning was that all might know Him—including Gentiles (Genesis 12:3).

 Read Romans 11:11. Why did salvation come to the Gentiles?

_____

_____

Israel's selfish, prideful actions and behaviors toward Gentiles was blatant sin against God. The effects of this sin pushed the Gentile people farther from God instead of drawing them closer to Him and caused a greater divide between the nations physically, socially, spiritually, and relationally. And because of Israel's sin and their rejection of God, He chose to make them jealous by opening His arms to the Gentiles.

Before we move forward, let's visualize these divides so we can see how they come together. Remember, we're dealing with two divides: one, the result of man's sin against God, the other a result of the sinful actions of God's people.

In the rectangle below write the word "God" at the top and the word "humankind" at the bottom. Now, write the word "Jew" on the left and the word "Gentile" on the right. Do you see the great divide between each one? Each divide is a result of sin. And each divide must be brought together.

Read Ephesians 2:13. Who was ultimately responsible for bringing the Gentile people to God? What was the avenue by which Gentiles were brought near to God?

_____

_____

Now with a red pen, in the center of the rectangle, write the word *JESUS* and connect God to humankind and Jew to Gentile.

In Ephesians 1:7, Paul reminds believers that in Christ they've been redeemed by His blood (NKJV), the only acceptable payment for their sins. Here in 2:11–13, not only does he remind believers of this again; he also says that it's the blood of Christ that brings us near to God and each other.

But why did it have to be blood that brought humankind back into right relationship with God

> Review Section 1, Lesson 2 on being redeemed by the blood.

83

and one another? Why not dinner and a movie? I mean, come on; how much easier would that have been?

Because dinner and a movie is surface and temporary and only costs about forty bucks. It doesn't seep into the deep places of our hearts. It doesn't last for a lifetime because it's not life-changing. And it's cheap!

" . . . for the blood is the life . . ."

-Deuteronomy 12:23 (NKJV)

Friends, without Christ we're dead. God is far off. And we walk this earth alone. The blood of Christ was a must! In blood is life and redemption and atonement, for it's the blood of Christ that seeps into the hidden crevices, pains, and sin-sickened spots of our hearts, reviving us from the inside. It's His blood that leads us from the shallows to the deep and enables us to live as one united force on the outside, partnering together to make Jesus known in our day.

 ### e. (embrace)

Do you have broken relationships right now due to sin in your life? Maybe the sin of pride has caused you to withdraw from others because you refuse to rejoice in their successes. Maybe a failure to forgive has driven a wedge between you and someone else. Maybe wanting someone else's gifts, talents, or blessings has caused your heart to be hard and ungrateful for the things God has given you.

Think about the shed blood of Christ. What does His spilled-out blood do for us and our relationships with God and one another? Give your messed-up, broken relationships to Him today. He is the

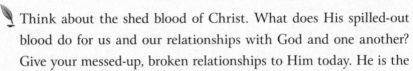

only One who can seep deep down into your heart, washing it clean, and unite you to your fellow man. Jot down your thoughts here.

_____

_____

_____

_____

_____

_____

The blood of Christ . . . It cleanses, heals,
redeems, and unifies.

d.i.v.e. into LESSON THREE

d. (define)

i. (investigate)

v. (visualize)

e. (embrace)

LESSON THREE

He Is Our Peace

Ephesians 2:14-22

Before you begin your time of study and learning, spend a few moments in prayer asking God to give you an open heart and mind to learn new truths from His Word.

v. (visualize)

Take a snapshot of Ephesians 2 by reading through the chapter at least three times, reminding yourself of the big picture. Also review your WOW from this chapter. Don't forget to add to your outline/paraphrase.

In this lesson we're going to zoom in on Ephesians 2:14–22. As you read these verses again, begin to d.i.v.e. below the surface.

WHAT IS PEACE?

Read Ephesians 2:14–18. According to verse 14, who is the embodiment of our peace?

_____

We learned in our last lesson that it's the blood of Christ that unites individuals to God and to each other. We also learned that sin is the cause of conflict and division. It is an enemy of peace.

d. (define)

Before we go any further, let's define peace again. In the space that follows, explain what you believe peace to be. (Look back at Section 1, Lesson 1 if you need to.)

_____

_____

_____

Webster's New World College Dictionary defines peace as, among other things, "freedom from war or a stopping of war," "a treaty or agreement to end war or the threat of war," and "an undisturbed state of mind; absence of mental conflict; serenity." Based on these definitions, we'd be correct in saying a time of peace is when wars cease to exist.

But, what does peace mean for the believer? What is spiritual peace, and which type of peace is more important? *The Holman Bible Dictionary* defines peace as "a sense of well-being and fulfillment that comes from God and is dependent on His presence."[1]

For the believer, peace is the inner calm that results from confidence in one's saving relationship with Christ. Peace is not related to circumstances, but rather, is based on knowing that all is well between oneself and God.

If this is what peace is for the believer, what is peace for the nonbeliever—the one who doesn't have assurance that all is well between himself and God?

Read Isaiah 59:8. Does an unbeliever travel the path of peace?

_____

No matter how hard you and I try to create peaceful situations on our own, without Christ in our midst, there is no peace. He IS our peace.

True peace comes only when one dies to self and that death is only a reality at the foot of the cross.

 ## BREAKING DOWN WALLS

God's peace breaks down the wall that separates enemies who would otherwise not fellowship with one another.

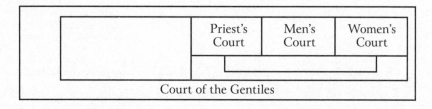

		Priest's Court	Men's Court	Women's Court
Court of the Gentiles				

Jews and Gentiles were separated physically, socially, spiritually, and relationally even when it came to worship. Gentiles weren't permitted to go beyond their designated area of worship in the temple. Between the Gentile court and the rest of the court of the Israelites a sign was hung that read:

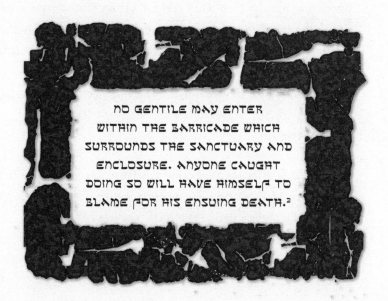

NO GENTILE MAY ENTER WITHIN THE BARRICADE WHICH SURROUNDS THE SANCTUARY AND ENCLOSURE. ANYONE CAUGHT DOING SO WILL HAVE HIMSELF TO BLAME FOR HIS ENSUING DEATH.[2]

Remember that God had separated the Jews and the Gentiles, not to make one group better than the other but for the purpose of saving both groups.

The Gentile court was meant to be a place of evangelism. **Read Mark 11:17.** Had this area been a place where nonbelievers were evangelized? What had it become?

_____

_____

Read Ephesians 2:15–17. What did Jesus destroy through His death on the cross? To whom did Peace come and to whom did Peace preach? Who were those that were "far away?" Who were those that were "near?"

_____

_____

When Jesus died on the cross, He broke down every barrier that divided humanity from God and God from humanity. He destroyed the ceremonial laws of feasts, sacrifices, and ordinances and all other "acts" that externally divided the nation of Israel from other nations. He did this for the purpose of creating in Himself "one new man" (NKJV) from the two.

 d. (define)

In Ephesians 2:16, Paul says that Christ reconciled both the Jew and the Gentile to God through the cross. Using a *Strong's Concordance* or *Webster's Dictionary* define the term *reconcile*.

_____

_____

_____

Thayer's Greek Definitions defines *reconcile* as "to bring back to a former state of harmony."[3]

Reconciliation is all about restoring broken relationships. In this passage we see spiritual and human reconciliation: Christ restoring both the Jews' and the Gentiles' relationship with God and bringing them together as one because peace with God brings about peace with one another.

Read Ephesians 2:18. What is the result of our reconciliation?

_____

_____

_____

I have no rights when it comes to finding favor with God or entering into His presence. My sin keeps me separated from the holiness of my Creator. But through Christ, I have and you have and every tribe and every nation has access to the God of the universe.

Christ's sacrificial death on the cross opened the door for us to experience intimate relationship with God. The Holy Spirit gently leads us into His presence. And the Father welcomes us all with open arms. What great beauty is found in the union of the Godhead that unites us all as one!

d.i.v.e. DEEPER . . . A STONE IN THE CORNER

Read Ephesians 2:19–22. What are some investigative questions you could ask of these verses? (See Appendix IV.)

_____

_____

_____

_____

---

d. (define)

Let's define the word *cornerstone* together. A cornerstone is a stone that forms the base of a corner of a building, joining together two walls. From the cornerstone, everything is built, structured, unified, supported, strengthened, and purposed.

"So" picture number 2.

> Remember
> *So* is a
> conjunctive
> adverb. It
> joins two
> clauses and
> shows cause
> and effect.

Remember our "so" picture number one? Here comes number two. In verses 14–18 Paul tells us Christ is our peace and has broken down the wall that separates Jew and Gentile, humankind and God, making us one in Him. "And so . . ." Paul says, we are "citizens with God's people, *members of God's holy family*, and residents of His household" (v. 19). And as a result, through Jesus the cornerstone, His church will be built.

In this building of His church, the Gospel message of the apostles and the prophets is the foundation upon which the building sits. Jesus is the cornerstone who perfectly, carefully, and purposefully is fitting together each living stone, building up His spiritual house as a dwelling place of God in the Spirit.

Like living stones, let yourselves be assembled
into a spiritual house, a holy order of priests
who offer up spiritual sacrifices that will be
acceptable to God through Jesus the Anointed.

-1 Peter 2:5

 e. (embrace)

In the last few lessons I've given you a lot of thoughts and directives in Scripture that could easily be tucked away as trivia. So, let's wrap up our time today embracing what we've learned and turning this trivia into tangible lessons.

Here's a quick recap of what we learned from Ephesians 2:

In Ephesians 2:1–3, we saw the life of the dead man walking, a life dead in trespasses and sins, lived according to "the course of this *perverse* world" and "the prince of the power of air."

In Ephesians 2:4–10, we saw how one is changed and made alive from the inside out because of the magnificent working of Christ on the cross.

In Ephesians 2:11–22, we saw the results of a life brought near by the blood of Christ, a life that is now unified with God and others.

In light of what we've learned, I feel it's a good time for us to embrace the question, **Do you know Jesus?**

Have you personally experienced God's grace? Have you been made alive in Him? Positionally, where are you? Are you in Christ or in this world? Are you in the shallows of religion or living from a place of deep faith? Are you dead, beating on your chest, trying to find purpose and meaning in this chaotic world? Do you *know* Jesus?

Before you answer, let me clarify my question. I don't mean, Do you know facts about Him, like when He lived, miracles He performed, or who His followers were? What I mean is, Do you know Him as your Friend? Your Savior and Lord? The only One who can give your life purpose and meaning?

I grew up in the church knowing a lot about the man Jesus, but never truly understanding who He was. I knew He lived a perfect life. I knew He healed the crippled and gave sight to those who couldn't see. I knew He was the Son of God, who died on the cross and rose again on the third day. I stood in the shallows of religion, longing for deep faith and intimate relationship with Jesus, but my mind couldn't grasp that He was for me!

It took me many years to come to the realization that the perfect life Jesus lived, the healing He offered, His death on the cross, and His rising again were to give my life purpose and meaning. It took many years to accept that Jesus was my salvation. That He *is* my salvation. And, my friend, He desires to be your salvation too.

Salvation is a gift from God. It's not something you and I can earn from doing good works, being a good person, or going to church. Salvation comes when one agrees with God that he or she has done wrong against Him, turns from a life of sin, acknowledges Jesus Christ as Lord, and believes His death, burial, and resurrection are for him or her.

I don't have all the answers, nor do I understand completely the immensity of God's grace toward me, but what I do know and believe with all my heart is this . . . *God loves you and me!* He loves us so much that He gave His Son's life for us. It took me a long time to believe Jesus loved me; I needed to see it for myself, over and over again. Maybe you're in the same boat. I encourage you to pull your Bible close and d.i.v.e. into all the verses I'm about to give you. I want you to *see* how much God loves you! **Read John 3:16.**

I also know . . . Our sin separates us from God; it hinders us from experiencing personal fellowship with Him. Sin condemns us to an eternity of being spiritually dead. But because of God's great love for us and His desire to be in relationship with us, He draws us, or calls us, to Himself, making us alive in Him through the shed blood of Christ. **Read John 6:44; Romans 3:23; 5:8; 6:23.**

Salvation—your relationship with God—begins with this: an understanding that you must be saved from your sin, an act being salvation of which we have no control over. **Read Ephesians 2:8–9.**

Repentance is key in salvation. But what *is* it exactly? Repentance is a complete mind and heart change. It is a deliberate turning away from a life of sin toward a holy God; it's stepping forward from the shallow into deep faith and relationship with Jesus. Peter preached repentance in Acts 2. Paul preached repentance over and over again in his letters to different churches. Far too often, I'm afraid, we gloss over this repentance element of salvation and, as we discussed earlier in our study, cling to easy believism instead. It's much easier to simply believe without that belief changing us from the inside out. But repentance is what God calls us to; there's no way around it. **Read Acts 26:18–20; 1 Thessalonians 1:9.**

Next, a confession from the mouth and a trust in the heart . . . Read Romans 10:9–10.

Scripture teaches we're to talk to God, to verbally admit to Him that we've sinned against Him and done things our way. Receiving His forgiveness and vocalizing our surrender to His leading are both very important.

I don't want to put words in your mouth, but talking to God for the first time can be a little scary. And I don't want you to think there's anything magical about this prayer, because if you're praying a prayer of surrender to Jesus, it's all about your heart and your desire to be in right relationship with Him.

I invite you to voice something like this to God if you're unsure how to talk to Him in this moment . . .

Jesus, I know that I'm a sinner. I know I've done wrong against You and am in need of salvation. Please forgive me of my sins. I repent of my sins, and desire with all my heart to turn from this life of sin to a life of abundant living in You. I lay my heart and life down before You as I confess with my mouth and believe in my heart that You are my Lord and Savior. Please create in me a clean and new heart. Dwell in my heart and help me to live my life in a manner that is pleasing to You. Thank You for Your sacrifice and for offering to me this free gift of salvation. Thank You for being my Lord and Savior. Amen.

If you've prayed with a heart of belief and surrender, then you've been made new in Christ; you've taken the first step from shallow religion toward deep faith and relationship with Jesus. Now it's time for you to begin growing in your relationship with God, Jesus, and the Holy Spirit.

Here are a few next steps to take:

1. Find a good Bible-based church that will disciple you and help you follow Jesus.

2. Get a Bible you can understand and start reading the book of John in the New Testament.

3. Begin having conversations with God, also known as *praying*. Prayer is simply chatting with God and is a way to connect you to His heart.

4. Remember: your relationship with God is a process of daily surrendering to Him and continuing to step forward into deep faith. Be patient in your new life journey, and surround yourself with people who can support you and help you.

Perhaps you've known Jesus for quite some time but find yourself stagnant in your relationship with Him; you find yourself still standing in the shallows. It could be that today finds you in a place of numbness toward God. Maybe circumstances have caused you to pull back instead of pressing into Him. It's possible that you've gotten so caught up in the performance of being a child of God that you've failed to sit and chat with Him over coffee, cultivating intimacy with your Savior.

Whatever this day holds for you and wherever you find yourself in your journey with God, I encourage you right now to sit with Him awhile. Pour out your heart. Praise Him. Thank Him. Confess sins, and ask for His strength to be unleashed in your life so that you experience victory over strongholds. Listen to Him. Allow God to love on you, heal you, and fill you up to overflowing. May His peace flood your soul and His love embrace your heart.

He's Got the Whole
World in His Hands ...
That Includes You

EPHESIANS THREE

d.i.v.e. into LESSON ONE

d. (define)

i. (investigate)

v. (visualize)

e. (embrace)

LESSON ONE

God's Mystery Made Known

Ephesians 3:1-13

 Before you begin your time of study and learning, spend a few moments in prayer asking God to give you an open heart and mind to learn new truths from His Word.

 ## v. (visualize)

Take a snapshot of Ephesians 3 by reading through the chapter at least three times so you understand the big picture. As you're reading, make note of any verse(s) that tugs at your heart; this may be the WOW God is giving you to embrace from chapter 3. Begin to develop your own outline/paraphrase.

In this lesson we're going to zoom in on Ephesians 3:1–13. As you read these verses again, begin to d.i.v.e. below the surface.

 ## PURSUING CONTENTMENT

Read Ephesians 3:1–7. Paul was physically imprisoned, but to whom did he consider himself to be spiritually enslaved?

_____

I don't think I was ever content. In the world's eyes, I had it all. A family that loved, cared for, and provided for my every need. Opportunities to go and do and be. A college education. Marriage. Children. On and on and on. I had it all in the palms of my hands, but it never seemed to be enough. Something was always missing.

And for years I searched for "it." I searched high and I searched low. I searched far and I searched near, but I could never find the elusive "it." I searched for "it" in one bad relationship after another. I searched in bags of chips and cartons of ice cream, and in frivolous shopping sprees that left my bank account in the negative. Through the clothes I wore, the things I said, and the way I presented myself to others, I searched for that thing, that feeling, that "it" that would give my life meaning and purpose.

But my life remained empty. And there was a deep hole in the depths of my being that was proof positive I was on the fast track to nowhere. Every day the bare, raw crevices of my heart screamed out, desiring to be filled. Oftentimes the shrills were deafening. Maddening. Overwhelmingly unbearable. My glass was not half-full, nor was it half-empty. My glass was shattered into a million tiny pieces, jagged shards of broken glass that cut and pierced and beckoned the crimson red blood in my veins to bubble to the surface.

My perspective was self. And my view of self was worthless. My pursuit of whatever this "it" was that would fill the shallowness that had taken up residence in my being left me carrying the weight of shame, guilt, worthlessness, heartache, and much pain.

Paul, imprisoned physically because of false accusations, was content with life because he could see it from God's perspective. He focused on what he was supposed to do, not on what he felt he should have done or what might be the more desirable situation. Paul was grateful for everything God had given him, the good, the bad, and the ugly. He had detached himself from the nonessentials in his life so he could concentrate on the eternal. His perspective was God and God alone.

Often, the desire for more or better possessions is really a longing to fill an empty place in our lives. Paul, however, had allowed God to fill him up, and because of that filling he had strength to withstand anything he came against: prison, beatings, rejection, loneliness.

 ## e. (embrace)

I wonder, are there empty places in your life today? With what are you trying to fill that emptiness: a job, an unhealthy relationship, money, food, drugs or alcohol, material possessions? In Psalm 81:10, the Lord says to open wide so that He can fill us full.

Friend, detach yourself from those nonessential things in your life so you can focus on the eternal, everlasting God and allow Him to fill you until your cup runs over. Stop what you're doing right now. Sit at His feet. Pour out your heart. (You may want to grab your prayer journal and let your heart words fill those pages.)

 ## d.i.v.e. DEEPER . . . A POSITIVE OUTLOOK

Paul hadn't been imprisoned so that others would marvel over how he endured the trial; he was imprisoned for the purpose of glorifying the Lord and preaching the Gospel to those he was commissioned to serve.

Read the following verses and record Paul's attitude and outlook on the task he'd been given.

Acts 20:17–24:

_____

_____

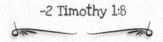

Acts 21:13:

_____

_____

2 Corinthians 1:3–7:

_____

_____

Colossians 1:24–29:

_____

_____

So don't be embarrassed to testify about our Lord
or for me, His prisoner. Join us in suffering for the
good news by the *strength* and power of God.

-2 Timothy 1:8

THE GREAT REVEALING

Remember, Paul wrote Ephesians as a letter, not as the "book" we
know. Chapter divisions and verse numbers were placed in the letter
much later to help us better digest the message. Letters flow, and
each paragraph or thought builds upon the last.

Paul begins chapter 3 with the words "for this reason" (NKJV). What
"reason" is he referring to?

_____

_____

Read Ephesians 3:1–2. To whom was Paul called to minister?

_____

Depending on the version of your Bible, you may find the word *message, administration, stewardship,* or *dispensation.*

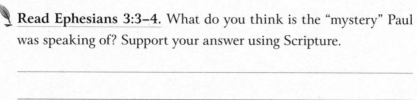

d. (define)

As I studied this passage, I was using the New King James Version, and before I could move forward in my study, I needed to define *dispensation.* Even if your version uses another word, I think this definition will shed greater light on what Paul wanted to share with us.

Thayer's Greek Definitions defines *dispensation (oikonomia)* as: "1) the management of a household or of household affairs; 1a) specifically, the management, oversight, administration, of other's property; 1b) the office of a manager or overseer, stewardship; 1c) administration, dispensation."[1]

Paul didn't choose his calling. By God's sovereign plan he was providentially chosen and gifted to be a minister, a steward, and an administrator of the Gospel to the Gentile people; and to extend to others the grace that had been lavished upon him (Ephesians 3:8; Acts 9:15).

Read Ephesians 3:3–4. What do you think is the "mystery" Paul was speaking of? Support your answer using Scripture.

_____

_____

Read Ephesians 3:5. Who was the agent by which and through whom God spoke to the prophets who penned the Scriptures?

_____

🖋 **Read 2 Peter 1:20–21.** Write the verses here. Do these verses support your previous answer?

_____

_____

_____

_____

🖋 **Read Ephesians 3:6.** In Ephesians 3:3, Paul mentions that a "mystery" had been made known to him. In verse 6, he reveals what this mystery is. What is it?

_____

_____

_____

Because of the blood of Christ, Jews and Gentiles are now on the same playing field. They're now spiritually equal, have the same spiritual inheritance, and are part of the same family. They are one in Christ.

🖋 **Read Ephesians 2:13 and 1 Corinthians 12:12–13.** What do these verses say about the mystery?

_____

_____

_____

🖋 **Read Ephesians 3:7 from the NKJV.** Who chose to make Paul a "minister"? (Hint: Ephesians 1:1 NKJV)

_____

_____

d. (define)

The New King James Version renders *servant and preacher* as "minister." Using a *Strong's Concordance*, define the term *minister*. Based on this definition, what would you say is a minister's primary responsibility?

_____

_____

A servant's primary responsibility is to do what he's told to do. Paul's primary responsibility was to serve God and do all God called him to do, easy or difficult.

According to Ephesians 3:7 and 1 Corinthians 15:10, is grace something that we deserve, or is it a gift?

_____

_____

There's no doubt God's grace is a gift that's completely undeserved by its recipient. God's grace makes us what we are. Paul's calling, his invitation to join God in His work, was initiated by the grace of God and sustained and carried out by the power of God.

PURPOSED GRACE

Read Ephesians 3:8. Why was God gracious toward Paul?

_____

_____

God's grace was given to Paul because, before the foundation of the world, he'd been handpicked to be an apostle among the Gentiles. Paul had a very clear and real understanding of God's righteousness, grace, and holiness. And because of this understanding, he was able to comprehend his own unrighteousness and in turn considered himself to be "the least of the least of the saints."

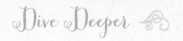

Read what he says in Galatians:

> But God—who set me apart even before birth and called me by His grace—chose, to His great delight, to reveal His Son in me so I could tell His story among the outsider nations. I didn't confer with anyone right away . . . But it quickly became obvious to them *what God was doing:* He had entrusted me to carry the good news to the uncircumcised, just as Peter was called to preach to those who were circumcised. God was at work in the ministry of Peter, as emissary to the Jews, and was also *moving and* working with me in my ministry to the outsider nations. (1:15–16; 2:7–8)

d.i.v.e DEEPER . . . UNSEARCHABLE RICHES

According to Ephesians 3:8, what was Paul to preach among the Gentiles?

_____

_____

What are the "unsearchable riches of Christ" that Paul speaks of in Ephesians 3:8 (NKJV)?

_____

_____

Read the following verses and record what they teach are the unsearchable riches of God and Christ. You may want to use the New King James Version for this exercise.

Romans 2:4

_____

_____

Ephesians 1:7

_____

_____

Ephesians 3:16

_____

_____

Colossians 1:27

_____

_____

Titus 3:4–7

_____

_____

God's "unsearchable riches" (NKJV) encompass all of His truths and all of His blessings and are riches He desires to lavish upon us, His children.

THE CHURCH TEACHES THOSE IN THE HEAVENLIES

Read Ephesians 3:9–11.

d. (define)

Using a *Strong's Concordance,* define the term *fellowship* as found in Ephesians 3:9 (NKJV).

_____

_____

_____

Based on Strong's definition of *fellowship* and your understanding of what the "mystery" that has been revealed is, what do you think Paul meant when he wrote, "To make all see what is the fellowship of the mystery, which from the beginning of the ages has been hidden in God who created all things through Jesus Christ" (NKJV)? (If you need a reminder of what the mystery is, review the previous lesson.)

_____

_____

_____

Let's go back to *The Voice* translation of Ephesians 3:9–11.

I am privileged to enlighten all *of Adam's descendants* to the mystery concealed from previous ages by God, the Creator of all, through Jesus the Anointed. *Here's His objective:* through the church, He intends now to make known His infinite and boundless wisdom to all rulers and authorities in heavenly realms. This has been His plan from the beginning, one that He has now accomplished through the Anointed One, Jesus our Lord.

Paul was chosen by God to make known the unification of Jew and Gentile believers as one in Christ. The purpose of this unification was to bring God glory and to display His magnificent wisdom and great power. God's eternal plan of salvation through Jesus Christ and the oneness of the body reaches farther than our finite minds can begin to understand.

Why God would choose to use the church to teach those who abide in the heavenly realms is a question that baffles my mind. But knowing He's using the church, of which I'm a part, to display His infinite and boundless wisdom to the unseen rulers and authorities humbles me and causes me to strive harder to live my life according to His divine purpose for me.

CONFIDENT ACCESS

Read Ephesians 3:12 from the New International Version:

In him and through faith in him we may approach God with freedom and confidence.

 In whom and through whom are we able to approach God? How are we to approach Him?

_____

_____

_____

 Write Hebrews 4:16 in the following space.

_____

_____

_____

 What does it mean to you to know you have personal access to God and can boldly approach Him at any time with anything?

_____

_____

_____

> Confident access is trust that knows no fear of rejection, because we belong to Him.
>
> -John MacArthur[2]

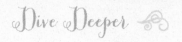

Read Ephesians 3:13. What was Paul's current "suffering" (The Voice) or "tribulation" (NKJV/NASB) or "trial" (NLT)? (Hint: Read Acts 28:16-31.)

_____

_____

How would Paul's suffering be to the benefit or honor of the Ephesian believers?

_____

_____

Paul was in a tough place. Prison, then or now, isn't glamorous, and I'm pretty sure he wouldn't have chosen it if he'd been given a say in the matter. But Paul was content with where God had him. He knew the situation he was in—every single bit of it—was God's intended purpose for his life at that moment. Why? Because God was using that imprisonment, that trial, that hard place, to draw the lost to Himself. He was working all things for His good pleasure and His great glory.

It's inevitable that in this life we're going to face situations that are hard to handle, events that blindside us, losses that knock us off our feet. It _is_ going to happen. The question is not when, but _how_ are we going to handle those trials when they come our way? Are we going to be content in the storm, trusting God to work _all_ things for our good and His glory? Are we going to accept the less-than-glamorous so His beauty is able to shine through? Are we going to "become discouraged," or allow our hearts to be yielded to God's perfect plan, even if it's a plan we wouldn't have chosen for ourselves? When we arrive on the other side of the trial, what will we do with the experience? Hide it, or share with others what God has led us through?

Rick Warren says in his book *The Purpose Driven Life:*

> It is [the] *painful* experiences . . . that God uses the most to pre-
> pare you for ministry. *God never wastes a hurt!* In fact, your great-
> est ministry will most likely come out of your *greatest* hurt. Who
> could better minister to the parents of a Down syndrome child
> than another couple who have a child afflicted in the same way?
> Who could better help an alcoholic recover than someone who
> fought that demon and found freedom? Who could better com-
> fort a wife whose husband has left her for an affair than a woman
> who went through that agony herself?
>
> God intentionally allows you to go through painful experi-
> ences to equip you for ministry to others . . .
>
> . . . The very experiences that you have resented or regret-
> ted most in life—the ones you've wanted to hide and forget—are
> the experiences God wants to use to help others. They *are* your
> ministry![3]

 e. (embrace)

We d.i.v.e. deeper into God's Word so He can d.i.v.e. deeper into
us. And sometimes the d.i.v.e. is painful all the way down to the
tips of our toes. But I've learned God is with me in the midst of my
pain, tenderly loving and working and healing, because someday,
somewhere, someone is going to need to hear my story of grace—not
because I'm a superstar but because my Jesus is.

The summer months found me serving as a youth intern in a local
church, teaching, ministering, and loving on kids who became an
important part of my life. The fall semester ushered in months of
studying through the Psalms in my Old Testament class and Paul's
Prison Epistles in New Testament class. I was happy. My heart was
full. I was in a good place.

But the heat of the summer months melted away to nothing, and
the coolness of the crisp fall air blew through so very quickly. And

there I was, in the dead of winter, broken, yet again, into a million pieces, heart cold and calloused, experiencing a death all its own.

We sat there, my friend and I, on the sidewalk outside the coffee shop, he numb from the icy-cold air, me numb from my shattered world. Coffee-shop music played in the background. Bells jingled each time the heavy glass door opened. People hurried in from the cold to warm their bodies with yummy deliciousness. They laughed and shrilled with glee. Some shared secrets and made grand plans. Others came to enjoy time alone away from the busyness of their lives.

It was almost like an out-of-body experience, if such a thing exists. I saw them all, the many who walked past. And I heard the music, the bell jingles, the laughter, and even the ahhs as the warmth of the patrons' treats made its way into their bellies. Yet, at the exact same time, I saw absolutely nothing and heard not a whisper. I was lost in an ocean of broken dreams; a sea of emptiness enveloped me. And years of innocence lost, wrongs done, and wounds inflicted welled up inside me.

The minutes passed by and turned into hours, how many exactly, I have no idea. My friend was the first one to speak.

"Ya know," he said, "God has a plan and reason for everything."

Immediately I felt a fire burn deep within. Slowly I turned my head, looked straight into his eyes, and loudly whispered my rage. "Do *not* play the Jesus card with me! Do you understand me? Do *not* tell me everything has a purpose and a plan. Are you f#*&^*$ kidding me?"

I stood to my feet, pacing back and forth, heart beating hard and loud, like a thousand bass drums. "Don't say that to me!" I screamed. "Don't!"

People stopped dead in their tracks to gawk at my public display of brokenness and pain.

"I can't do this!" I went on. "Do you know how bad this hurts? I can't breathe. I can't think. I can't feel. Except . . . I feel everything. And my mind races. It wasn't supposed to be this way. It wasn't supposed to end like this. It wasn't supposed to end at all!"

A madwoman walking is what I was. I mumbled. I screamed obscenities. I cried; no, I wailed in pain. I lashed out at my friend in unimaginable ways. He sat there, silent.

As I paced with fists clenched, the tears poured from my eyes. The pain, the ache, the emptiness inevitably forced me to my knees. My friend came to my side, trying to ease the burden, to lighten the load of pain that weighed me down because years of hurts and heartaches and things that should never happen to anyone had just broken me.

"Don't touch me!" I shouted. "Don't touch me! Please don't touch me!" I cried uncontrollably, hugging my waist, my head lying against the gravel parking lot.

But my friend didn't listen. He lifted me up from my puddle of pain so I could see into his eyes.

"I will play the Jesus card," he said, "because it's the winning card. And the pain you feel right now will one day subside. And you'll be able to stand, victorious over this emptiness you feel."

That was 1998. The pain I felt that cold winter night, the ache that left my heart empty, didn't vanish in a few short days; it took years. Years of God working and me surrendering. Years of God healing and me accepting His healing and realizing there was purpose for my pain.

But I need you to know something; those years found me broken many more times by the weight of pains. They also found me searching to be accepted. Searching to be loved. Searching to be heard. Searching for the real me. And my search led me from one unhealthy relationship to the next, from one bottle of alcohol to another, and from one shopping spree to the next door-buster sale. During those years I married and had my first child, but I still searched for more. My searching and pain dead-ended in a courtroom, with me uttering a word I never thought I'd utter: "Guilty."

I then found myself in an extremely dark place for two years. On a daily basis I contemplated taking my life; I'd attempted it years before, but this time I knew I wouldn't fail. I emotionally disconnected from my daughter and husband; I felt nothing for them. I was out all hours of the night, driving dark roads, sitting in empty parking lots, hiding from the world because I was so very ashamed of what I'd become.

Driven face to the ground once again, like Paul, I had my own Damascus road experience. And once again my heart screamed out as tears poured from my eyes, *God, I'm a mess. I'm a complete and utter failure. I'm stupid. I'm used up. I'm alone. I hate myself. And believe me when I tell You, You want nothing to do with me! I'm sure there are others far less complicated than me. Others who are better suited and much more deserving than me to be Your child.*

My insides were jacked up. I'd been deeply wounded by others and myself. And my wounds were bleeding and festering and stunk to high heaven. I had absolutely nothing to offer God. There were no credentials to my name. No great accolades or endorsements to cause heads to turn my way. I was just a confused, shame-filled, broken-down girl.

But God had purpose for my pain.

The day God chose me and turned my insides upside down and right side out, the day He turned my unlikeliness into something extraordinary in His book, I was a hot mess. But today I stand changed from the inside out only because the Word of God has rocked me to the core, healing the wounds that left me empty and lonely. I stand brave, not fearful. I stand whole, not broken.

For those of you who are hurting today, weighed down by an oversized load of pain, heartache, hurt, and complete emptiness, may I lay the Jesus card on the table and say to you, *"God has a plan and reason for all your pain"*?

It's okay if you can't see His plan and purpose right now through your pain; and it's okay if you scream obscenities at me. And while the perception may be that you're "the perfect Jesus girl," the reality may be that you're standing in a very different, very wounded place this very moment. People may not see that, but Jesus does. It's okay. You don't have to be who others think you should be. It's okay for you to feel your pain. But what's not okay is for you to stay buried by it, broken down in a puddle of hurt and heartache.

The time will come, and for each of us it's different, when you'll have to look your friend Jesus in the face, choose to allow Him to lift you above the pain, and embrace the healing He offers. The day will come when you'll have to lay it all at His feet and allow Him to carry the load of your heartache. Until that day comes, even if you're only able to know this in your head, know that God is actively working, there is purpose for your pain, and one day, you'll stand on the other side of it, sharing your grace story for His honor and glory.

We are confident that God is able to orchestrate everything to work toward something good and beautiful when we love Him and accept His invitation to live according to His plan.

-Romans 8:28

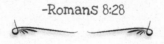

d.i.v.e. into LESSON TWO

d. (define)

i. (investigate)

v. (visualize)

e. (embrace)

Worship the Lord

Ephesians 3:14-21

Before you begin your time of study and learning, spend a few moments in prayer asking God to give you an open heart and mind to learn new truths from His Word.

v. (visualize)

Take a snapshot of Ephesians 3 by reading through the chapter at least three times, reminding yourself of the big picture. Is there a WOW you're embracing and implanting in your heart? Take a few moments to review that verse(s). Don't forget to add to your outline/paraphrase.

In this lesson we're going to zoom in on Ephesians 3:14–21. As you read these verses again, begin to d.i.v.e. below the surface.

BOWING THE KNEE

 Read Ephesians 3:14. Where have you read the phrase "for this reason" before? (Hint: See the last lesson, under the heading "The Great Revealing.") Why do you think Paul began these verses in a similar fashion?

_____

_____

Bowing the knee represents a reverence and respect for God; it's one of the many postures of worship.

Paul repeats the phrase "for this reason" from Ephesians 3:1 (NKJV) because in verse 1 he paused to talk about the body of Christ, the mystery, and his ministry of sharing the mystery. He's now picking up where he left off.

Paul bows his knees before his heavenly Father as he makes his request known. He prays that the Ephesian believers, as well as all believers, would be enabled by God to use the power that already dwells within them through the working of the Holy Spirit.

i. (investigate)

Let's look more into the posture of worship.

When God told Moses in Exodus 3:6, "I am the True God, *the God* of your father, the God of Abraham, Isaac, and Jacob," Moses knew he was in the presence of the Lord, Yahweh, the Great I AM.

Read the second half of Exodus 3:6. What was Moses' response to being in the presence of God?

_____

_____

God had already told Moses to take off his shoes because the place where he stood was holy ground. But when Moses realized he was in the presence of the Lord, he hid his face, a reaction showing reverent fear and proper respect for God.

How are we to react in the presence of the Lord? How do we demonstrate proper respect and reverence for the Lord, the Great I AM? Does one always have to bow his knee before God, take off his shoes, or hide his face? Is a bowing of the knee more important than a bowing of the heart? Let's d.i.v.e. deeper into these questions together.

Read 2 Chronicles 20:18. How did Jehoshaphat worship the Lord?

_____

_____

_____

Read Nehemiah 8:5–6. What was the people's outward response to the reading of God's Word?

_____

_____

_____

Now let's search out our *thoughts* and ways and return to the Eternal. Now let's lift up to God in heaven our hearts along with our hands *in praise and supplication*.

-Lamentations 3:40-41

I understand there are those who aren't comfortable with lifting their hands to the Lord and those who can't physically prostrate themselves before Him. In Lamentations 3:41, Jeremiah tells us to "lift up . . . our hearts" to the Lord.

 ## I SAT IN THE CORNER

The temperature read a frigid 17 degrees. Shards of ice blanketed the windshield. The air blew cold around my frame.

But my heart? It was ablaze. Burning with anticipation for what the impending hours would bring—hours of worship, glorious, beautiful worship. Its beauty would abound all the more when partnered with the family of God joined as one because of One.

As we reached our destination, I saw that others had also come, many, in fact. They'd come to worship. Or maybe they'd come in search of that *something* that their heart desperately longed for or possibly wasn't yet aware of. But either way, whatever the reason . . . they'd come. And I prayed their hearts would never be the same. I prayed *my* heart would never be the same.

Melodies. Choruses. Harmonies. The room, our warehouse, the shell that hugs the body of Christ, was filled with voices lifting high the name of Jesus.

Glorious, beautiful worship.

Hundreds upon hundreds gathered as God's servant stood to proclaim the magnificent Word of God. Except we didn't sit. We couldn't sit, because there were no chairs. No place to cradle our frames.

We were led to a corner in the back of the warehouse. And we sat. On the floor. And we listened to the living Word of God as it was spoken.

And he said to all, "If anyone would come after me, let him deny himself and take up his cross daily and follow me. For whoever would save his life will lose it, but whoever loses his life for my sake will save it.

-Luke 9:23-24 (ESV)

Becoming like Jesus is not a deed, it's a death. It's complete self-denial.

-Jimmy Carroll

Following Jesus is surrender. And the surrendering is never complete this side of glory, but still we're called to it—daily. It is the mission. It is worship.

Positionally, as a child of God, I am always in Christ. But, practically I must daily remain in His presence.

Abide in me, and I in you. As the branch cannot bear fruit by itself, unless it abides in the vine, neither can you, unless you abide in me. I am the vine; you are the branches. Whoever abides in me and I in him, he it is that bears much fruit, for apart from me you can do nothing.

-John 15:4-5 (ESV)

What I want to accomplish in my flesh can only be accomplished in my death.

-Jimmy Carroll

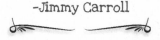

To be like Jesus I must die to self. My rebirth, my revival from the dead, must be a life lived in Jesus, for Jesus. I must surrender.

Now standing in the corner to which we'd been led, I was oblivious to the hundreds that surrounded me. It was our corner now. It was our warehouse now. God's and mine. No one else's. And I surrendered.

I surrendered my will, my dreams, and my plans. I surrendered it all. I will daily follow after His will. I will daily live out His dreams for me. And I will daily accomplish His plan for my life.

I will surrender. Daily. It is my heart worship.

I am no longer my own but yours. Put me to what you will, rank me with whom you will; let me be employed for you or laid aside for you, exalted for you or brought low by you; let me have all things, let me have nothing: I freely and wholeheartedly yield all things to your pleasure and disposal. And now, glorious and blessed God, Father, Son, and Holy Spirit, you are mine and I am yours. And the covenant now made on earth, let it be ratified in heaven. Amen.

–John Wesley[1]

Our posture before the Lord has everything to do with the attitude and surrender of our hearts in our worship of Him. Our hearts can be lifted to and prostrated before the Lord at the same time in respect, reverent fear, and complete surrender to who He is.

 e. (embrace)

How long has it been since you lifted up and prostrated your heart before the Lord? Stop now and worship Him for who He is, whether that's through the bowing of your knees, the lifting of your hands, or the lying on your face before Him. Surrender your dreams, and embrace God's plan for your life. Submit to His leading. Give Him the respect and reverence He rightly deserves.

HE IS OUR FATHER

Read Ephesians 3:15 from the Amplified Bible:

> For Whom every family in heaven and on earth is named [that Father from Whom all fatherhood takes its title and derives its name.]

Who is the originator of family?

_____

God is a beautiful, complete picture of what a father should be. He is loving, compassionate, accepting, forgiving, gracious, merciful, gentle, protective, and disciplinarian when needed.

Paul had no fear of God the Father; instead he felt great comfort and confidence in being able to approach his heavenly Father. He knew God would never lead him into a situation where He wouldn't be right there by his side, leading and guiding. Paul also knew that there was nothing that could pull him from his Father's care and protection.

Read John 10:27–30, and write these verses in your own words.

_____

_____

_____

_____

_____

One of a child's strongest needs is for a father's protection. Yet not everyone has experienced the protection of an earthly father. But, precious one, you can be secure in the arms of your heavenly Father and know that He'll always provide protection and love for you. His arms are big enough to hold each and every one of us. He'll never abandon us or allow anyone to take us from Him.

 e. (embrace)

By being secure in our Father's arms, we can learn to take the risks that faith requires. Have you been afraid to take that next step of faith, resisting something new God has for your life? You can rest

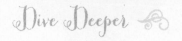

assured that God will not call you where He cannot lead you and protect you. So what's that new thing God is calling you to? Put it to paper and pray that you would be brave and step out and do it for Jesus.

_____

_____

_____

GOD'S GREAT POWER

Read Ephesians 3:16–21. In these five verses Paul, once again, prays for the Ephesian believers and all believers who will come after them.

Note what John MacArthur says concerning Paul's prayer in his commentary on Ephesians: "Paul is not praying for God to *give* these **riches** to believers, but **that He would grant** believers **to be strengthened** by God **according** to the **riches** they already possess. He wants them to live lives that correspond to the spiritual wealth they have in Christ."[2]

Paul's desire is that believers unleash within them the spiritual wealth they received through the indwelling of the Holy Spirit at the moment of salvation. He doesn't pray for anything new; he prays that what they already possess be recognized and lived out.

Let's break down these verses together, noting what Paul prays for every believer.

Paul prays for . . .

ONE: _____ (Ephesians 3:16).

Paul prays for the inner man to grow stronger through and because of the power of the Holy Spirit working in him. He prays for the limitless riches of God to strengthen the spirit of the believer, enabling him to live out his intended purpose.

Read the following verses. What do they say about the inner man and how he should be growing in his walk?

Acts 1:8

_____

_____

Romans 12:1–2

_____

_____

2 Corinthians 4:16

_____

_____

Galatians 5:16

_____

_____

TWO: _____ (Ephesians 3:17).
Paul prays that the result of Christ making His home within the heart of the inner man be a foundation of love.

d. (define)

Define the following terms as found in Ephesians 3:17 (NKJV).

Dwell

_____

_____

Rooted

_____

_____

Grounded

_____

_____

What do you think it means to be "rooted and grounded in love" (NKJV)?

_____

_____

_____

I'm a daddy's girl; I always have been. When I was little, I looked forward to hunting season because it was our special time. I have many hunting trip memories tucked away—adventures had, miles walked, sights seen—but one particular trip outweighs them all.

My dad, granddaddy, and I loaded up the truck one Friday afternoon and headed north for an overnight camping/hunting trip. When we arrived at our campsite, they pitched the tent and I "set up" the kitchen. We then gathered firewood, started our fire, and sat around in lawn chairs, eating ham sandwiches and drinking RC Cola. They told stories and laughed until they cried; I smiled and asked questions and enjoyed being with "my guys."

I couldn't sleep that night because I was so excited about the next day's adventure; waking up early and hiking through the woods was a thrill. But when morning came, my seven-year-old body was completely exhausted. Dad promised he'd find me a place to sleep, but I had to get up; he couldn't leave me alone at the campsite. So I reluctantly dressed in my camos and our adventure began.

We walked for what seemed like a thousand miles before stopping in front of a very large, skyscraper kind of tree. It was the kind of tree that required a two-person hug, if you know what I mean. All around the base, its enormous roots broke through the ground beneath.

"This is good," my dad said. "You can take a nap here while we hunt."

Between the large roots was the "here" he was referring to. So, I snuggled myself between those roots and slept while my dad and granddaddy hunted. But as I lay there before falling asleep, I remember looking up into the morning sky and watching the branches of the tree sway back and forth as the wind blew. Glancing to my left and right, I felt safe, like I was wrapped in a hug between those roots.

That skyscraper tree was rooted deep, grounded and stable in the earth in which it'd been planted. It had grown tall and it had grown wide. It stood out among the other trees, so much so that it was the one my dad chose to be my resting place while he hunted.

We, the church, should be the "tree" others choose as their resting place, their safety, their hug of healing and encouragement. We should be rooted deep, grounded and stable in the love of Jesus, growing up strong, and reaching far and wide to those around us. Paul prayed it over us; I pray it over us, over me! *Lord, may I be rooted deep in Your love, reaching far and wide to those You've placed in my life. May it be, Lord, may it be!*

THREE: _____ (Ephesians 3:18).

Paul prays that in whatever spiritual direction a believer looks, he will be able to see God's love.

 **Read Ephesians 2:11–18.** What is the width of God's love?

_____

Read Ephesians 1:4–5. What is the length of God's love?

_____

Read Ephesians 1:3; 2:6. What is the height of God's love?

_____

Read Ephesians 2:1–3. What is the depth of God's love?

_____

FOUR: _____ (Ephesians 3:19).

Paul prays that believers will know the love of Christ in ways they've never known it before.

To know Christ's love takes us beyond our own human knowledge. His agape love is infinitely great and divinely given. God's love is based on who He is; therefore, it's everlasting, unlike human love. Man's love loves for what it can get. God's love loves for what it can give.

For God expressed His love for the world in this way: He gave His only Son so that whoever believes in Him will not face everlasting destruction, but will have everlasting life.

–John 3:16

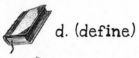

d. (define)

Using a *Strong's Concordance*, define the term *filled* as found in Ephesians 3:19 in the New King James Version.

_____

_____

_____

Consider how Thayer's Greek Definitions defines *filled* as found in Ephesians 3:19.

1) to make full, to fill up, i.e. to fill to the full; 1a) to cause to abound, to furnish or supply liberally; 1a1) I abound, I am liberally supplied; 2) to render full, i.e. to complete[3]

What do you think it means to "be filled with all the fullness of God"?

_____

_____

_____

To be filled with all the fullness of God means that one is completely dominated by Him. In order to be filled with God, one must be emptied of self. One must deny self and take up one's cross and follow hard after Jesus.

SO MANY AWE-INSPIRING THINGS

Now . . .

Now to the God who can do so many awe-*inspiring things,*
immeasurable things, things greater than we ever could
ask or imagine through the power at work in us, to Him
be all glory in the church and in Jesus the Anointed from
this generation to the next, forever and ever. Amen.

-Ephesians 3:20-21

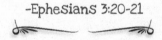

I don't know about you, but I just need to stop right here, stand
to my feet, and get my praise on for a moment. Care to join me?

If there's ever anything in Scripture that gets me fired up, it's
these two verses. We could camp out here for a month of Sundays
and still not unpack every ounce of truth contained in Paul's words.

Look back at the verses leading up to this treasure and see the
progression of God mightily working through them all . . .

When the Holy Spirit has strengthened us with His power
(v. 16), Christ has taken up residence in our hearts (v. 17), and God
has filled us with His fullness (v. 19), then what God will be able to
do in and through us will be beyond anything our finite minds can
comprehend. Can I get an "Amen!" And here's the beautiful thing:
We don't have to sit around waiting for the "when" to come. Paul
tells us the "when" is NOW.

Now is the time for each and every one of us to consider and
contemplate the magnificent ability of our God. In the first nine-
teen verses of Ephesians 3, Paul outlined for us what would appear
to be impossible—the unity of Jews and Gentiles, making them one
in Christ. Now, in verses 20 and 21, he's going to show us how an

impossible situation can be made possible in and through the power of God Almighty.

Check this out! "Now," Paul says, is the time for us to turn our attention to the One who can: "Now to the God who can." Do you know that God *can*? He can move mountains. He can calm seas. He can create man from the dust of the earth—and raise dead men from the grave. He can cause the blind to see and the lame to walk. And God can mend the broken heart and redeem the wayward soul. He can piece back together what's been broken and give back what's been taken. There's absolutely nothing that God can't do. He *can*!

And not only can He do a few things; He can "do so many *awe-inspiring things, immeasurable things,* things greater than we ever could ask or imagine." Remember from the beginning of our study the life Paul lived, the life God rescued him from? Paul knew that he'd not only been called out of a life of sin, but that he'd been called to abundant living, to live in the "immeasurably more" of God.

Read John 10:10, and then write it here.

_____

_____

_____

Jesus doesn't save us only to rescue us from an eternity in hell. He saves us from a life of sin so that we can experience a showering down of His peace, joy, mercy, grace, love, healing, freedom, and purpose upon our lives. He rescues us so that we can experience the abundance of His goodness as we live deeply in Him.

Let me try to explain this abundant life . . .

Abundant is a translation of the Greek word *perissos.* It means "exceeding some number or measure or rank or need, over and above, more than is necessary, super added, exceeding abundantly, supremely something further, more, much more than all."[4]

When Jesus said He came to give us life with joy and abundance, He meant for the believer who'd said yes to His calling and surrendered to follow hard after Him to be blessed exceedingly, abundantly, much more, beyond, beyond anything our minds can even begin to grasp.

My church sponsors an orphanage in Uganda. Several years ago an offering was taken to build housing for the orphanage. Over a period of weeks, many sacrificially gave above and beyond their tithes, and the money was raised for the first phase of the orphanage to be built.

Some months later, our pastor shared that the orphanage was at a place of immediate need to begin on the next phase of building so that more children could be taken care of. The elders of the church gathered and prayed and came to the congregation with what they felt led of God for our church to do.

What they felt God calling us to do was this: On April 10, 2011, all the monies given would go to the orphanage in Uganda. Nothing would be received into the church's budget for that week. Every penny would go to Uganda. Their goal was that we raise $50,000. This amount of money was a huge step of faith for our elders to cast vision for because that was more than our normal weekly offerings. It was an abundant amount for our church to give.

April 10 came and went. We believed God for abundant blessings that day. But we didn't raise $50,000.

We raised $135,000!

God raised $135,000. He gave immeasurably more than our minds could begin to grasp.

Above and beyond. More than we could even conceive. Beyond our wildest dreams.

That is the abundant life. That is where God wants us. He doesn't want us settling for the $50,000, if you will; He desires that we live in the realm of exceeding abundance, above all that we can think to ask for or even begin to imagine.

The time is now for us to set our gaze upon the One who can do so many *awe-inspiring things, immeasurable things,* things greater than we ever could ask or imagine with the impossible in our lives. And the time is now for us to unleash the power that dwells within.

DYNAMITE POWER

d. (define)

Using a *Strong's Concordance,* define the term *power* as found in Ephesians 3:20.

_____

_____

_____

From the Greek word *dunamis* (power) comes the English word *dynamite.* When ignited, dynamite has the potential to literally blow to pieces its intended target. Can you imagine how different our lives would be if we lived in the power of the Holy Spirit? We live with His mighty power within us every day, but do we walk in that power? Do we blow to pieces the traps Satan sets because we fight in God's power? Do we climb mountains of tribulations and stand victorious because God's power enables us to keep placing one foot in front of the other?

Sadly, and far too often, we forget about the magnificent power that indwells us. I lived for years—as a believer, mind you—standing in the shallows, failing to tap into and unleash the power of the Holy Spirit. My problem wasn't that I didn't believe God could; my problem was I didn't believe God could do *awe-inspiring things, immeasurable things* greater than all I asked or thought of *for me.* I limited

Him within my own little world. "How?" you ask. I limited God by all the church knowledge with which I'd filled my mind throughout my growing-up years. I limited Him by knowing Him only by extension of my parents' relationship with Him. I limited God by being so set in my ways that my denominational background was the only one that was right.

And because I limited God and His Holy Spirit's power at work in me, I never believed He was really for me. I believed He could do *awe-inspiring things, immeasurable things* in the lives of those around me, but I didn't believe He could or would do that for me.

It all came down to a choice: to believe God was able to do the impossible and unleash the power of the Holy Spirit in my life, or continue to hinder His work in my life.

I chose to believe God, and my life has never been the same.

Do you see how this all works together? How Paul's words all build upon each other? How *now* is the time to turn to the only One who can do immeasurably more than our finite minds can even begin to comprehend through the mighty power of the Holy Spirit working in our lives?

As we wrap up this lesson, I want to leave you with what I think is one of the most beautiful things about today's passage. Remember, Paul was in prison when he penned the book of Ephesians. But even in prison, he knew his God could do things greater than he could ever imagine. Paul's complete, absolute, unwavering faith in God enabled him to write these words of praise, expressing the glory of God in Ephesians 3:20–21.

In his impossible situation, Paul was still able to praise because his God *could*. Maybe today finds you in what you believe to be an impossible situation: a failing marriage, a wayward child, job loss, financial ruin, years of addiction, feelings of guilt and shame over past sins . . . the list could go on and on. My friend, the time is *now*! Right now, in this very moment, it's time for you to turn your attention to the One who can make your impossible possible, the One who can do *awe-inspiring things, immeasurable things,* things greater than your mind can even begin to fathom.

 ## e. (embrace)

Can I challenge you to do one thing today in closing? In your impossible, choose to praise. Praise the One who holds your life in His hands. Praise the One who has so many awe-inspiring, immeasurable things in store for you. Just as Paul sat physically imprisoned but spiritually free when he wrote this praise, will you choose today to unleash the power of the Holy Spirit in your life and stand spiritually free as you write out your own words of praise to the One who *can*?

We've talked a lot over the last two lessons about the purpose of our pains and seemingly impossible situations. Each of us faces mountains to climb and valleys to travel through. Our lives are fraught with severed relationships, broken hearts, and pasts that want to invade and haunt our present. Maybe you're facing an impossible situation today. Maybe He's asking you to lay your pain at His feet. My friend, believe God to do the impossible. Trust He'll do exceedingly abundantly beyond your wildest dreams. His Word says He can!

Right now grab an index card, piece of paper, napkin . . . it doesn't matter what it is; just grab something you can write on. Jot down this truth and carry it with you today. Tonight, before you go to bed, tape it to your bathroom mirror so in the morning it's the first thing you see . . .

Now to the God who can do so many *awe-inspiring things,*
immeasurable things, things greater than we ever could
ask or imagine through the power at work in us, to Him
be all glory in the church and in Jesus the Anointed from
this generation to the next, forever and ever. Amen.

-Ephesians 3:20-21

So Happy Together

EPHESIANS FOUR

d.i.v.e. into LESSON ONE

d. (define)

i. (investigate)

v. (visualize)

e. (embrace)

From Knowledge to Action

Ephesians 4:1-16

Before you begin your time of study and learning, spend a few moments in prayer asking God to give you an open heart and mind to learn new truths from His Word.

v. (visualize)

Take a snapshot of Ephesians 4 by reading through the chapter at least three times so you understand the big picture. As you're reading make note of any verse(s) that tugs at your heart; this may be the WOW God wants you to embrace from chapter 4. Begin to develop your own outline/paraphrase.

In this lesson we're going to zoom in on Ephesians 4:1–16. As you read these verses again, begin to d.i.v.e. below the surface.

SCALPEL, PLEASE!

I was pumped. We'd been studying for weeks: reading books, listening to lectures and taking notes, taking pop quizzes and chapter tests, and working out strategies with our lab partners as to who would do what, when, and how.

Finally the day came. I remember waking up earlier than usual and beaming with excitement. There was no piddling around for me that morning, no hitting the snooze button on my alarm. I was up and at 'em, showered, dressed, backpack filled, waiting on my best friend, who was normally waiting on me.

I don't think her car had come to a complete stop before I pulled open the door, threw my stuff in the backseat, and plopped down beside her. We looked at each other, both grinning from ear to ear, and squealed. Who would have ever thought two sixteen-year-old girls would be so excited to dissect a frog, a cow's eye, and a piglet?

When the bell for third period biology rang, we—actually every junior in our class—speed walked to the lab. Ms. B greeted us at the door like she always did, but I could tell even she was thrilled for today's class.

I met up with my lab partner at our station, and we high-fived. On the tabletop sat our aprons and a box ful of tools: scalpels, small scissors, tweezers, a dissecting tray, paper towels, gloves, safety glasses, pins, and a plastic bag.

Because we'd been studying and making notes for weeks, we knew exactly what needed to be done. First, put on aprons, safety glasses, and then gloves. Check. We looked ridiculous, but we didn't care. Next, place a few paper towels on the table and then lay out all the dissecting tools. Done. And last, place the dissecting tray in the center of the table and wait. Check. Everything was done. It was all ready.

The room was buzzing with anticipation (and a few upset tummies) as Ms. B rolled her cart around and passed out specimens, the cow's eye, then the frog, then the piglet. She walked back to the front of the lab, clenched her hands together in front of her, smiled, and said, "Students, for weeks we've studied and you've learned everything you need to know to dissect these specimens. You know the things you're looking for and you have the tools you need. It's time for you to put into practice what you've learned. Have fun!"

And with those words said, it was time! I looked at my partner and said, "Scalpel, please!"

In the first half of Paul's letter, he, like Ms. B, has laid it all out for us; he's reminded us and we have listened and remembered. We've remembered the reality of life without Christ, dead in trespasses and sins. We've remembered our former position: in the world, controlled by the enemy of God; in life, separated from others and without hope. We've remembered God awakening us to new life in Christ because of His selfless sacrifice of accepting God's wrath in our place. We've remembered that we've been chosen and set apart to be ministers of the Gospel of grace, sharing with others our story of redemption. And we've remembered that we've been united as one, many individuals making up the body of Christ.

I can picture Paul standing before the class, hands clenched in front of him, smiling as he begins the last half of this letter. "I, therefore . . ." (NKJV). *Therefore*, like *so*, which we discussed in earlier lessons, is a conjunctive adverb joining two clauses and showing cause and effect. Our time of reading about and remembering the inside knowledge of faith and salvation (chapters 1–3) has come to an end. It's time to pick up the proverbial scalpel and embrace our new position in Christ; it's time to let our inside transformations of deeper faith in Jesus become evident to others who may still be standing in the shallows and those who are diving deeper alongside us (chapters 4–6).

Read Ephesians 4:1–6 from the New King James Verison..

Begin your d.i.v.e. today by reading and breaking down Ephesians 4:1 into bite-size pieces. As you pull out key phrases, define

words and ask investigative questions of each phrase (hint: you should have at least three pieces to chew on).

1._____

2._____

3._____

As I dove deeper into this verse, reading my commentaries and study notes in my Bible, I kept coming across the same thing. All my teachers were telling me that the literal translation of the phrase "prisoner of the Lord" reads "prisoner in the Lord." Did you see it? No? Read the literal translation again.

"prisoner in the Lord."

See it that time? Still no? Let me show you from an interlinear Bible.

◄ **Ephesians 4:1** ►

Ephesians 4 Interlinear

3870 [e]	3767 [e]	4771 [e]	1473 [e]	3588 [e]	1198 [e]	1722 [e]	2962 [e]	516 [e]	4043 [e]	3588 [e]	2821 [e]
Parakalō	oun	hymas	egō	ho	desmios	en	Kyriō	axiōs	peripatēsai	tēs	klēseōs
1 Παρακαλῶ	οὖν	ὑμᾶς ,	ἐγὼ	ὁ	δέσμιος	ἐν	Κυρίῳ ,	ἀξίως	περιπατῆσαι ,	τῆς	κλήσεως
exhort	therefore	you	I	the	prisoner	in	[the] Lord	worthily	to walk	of the	calling
V-PIA-1S	Conj	PPro-A2P	PPro-N1S	Art-NMS	N-NMS	Prep	N-DMS	Adv	V-ANA	Art-GFS	N-GFS

3739 [e]	2564 [e]
hēs	eklēthēte
ἧς	ἐκλήθητε ;
to which	you were called
RelPro-GFS	V-AIP-2P

Image taken from BibleHub.com. Used with Permission

An interlinear Bible shows the Hebrew and Greek text of the Old and New Testaments alongside the English translation.

Paul says he's a prisoner *in the Lord*, not a prisoner in Rome, or a prisoner in chains, but a prisoner in the Lord. His spiritual position took precedence over his physical reality. And from the spiritual position of being *in* Jesus, he lived unshaken by present circumstances.

Honored to be bound to Jesus, the One who'd rescued him from a life of darkness, breathing new life into his being, he encourages believers to "walk worthy of the calling with which you were called" (NKJV). This "calling" is God's calling of His elect to salvation and lifetime service and carries the responsibility of deep faith living. As was the case with Paul, may our spiritual positions take precedence over our physical realities. And from the spiritual position of being in Jesus, may we live deeply and walk worthy of our callings, unshaken by present circumstances.

d. (define)

 Use a *Strong's Concordance* to define *walk* as found in Ephesians 4:1. Then, based on that definition, write in your own words what you believe it means for believers to walk worthy of the calling to which they've been called.

_____

_____

Read 2 Timothy 1:9 and write it here.

_____

_____

Does your outside living reflect your inside transformation? In other words, does your walk equal your talk? Are you living worthy of the calling to which you've been called? Not exactly sure? Let's look at the characteristics of a worthy walk and then come back to this question.

CHARACTERISTICS OF A WORTHY WALK

Read Ephesians 4:2–3. List the 5 characteristics of a worthy walk mentioned in these verses.

1._____

2._____

3._____

4._____

5._____

ONE: Humility is foundational to Christian living. Christ beautifully set the example of humble living by the way He lived His life.

But He poured Himself out *to fill a vessel brand new;* a servant in form and a man indeed. The very likeness of humanity, He humbled Himself, obedient to death–a merciless death on the cross!

-Philippians 2:7-8

"Put My yoke upon your shoulders–*it might* appear heavy at first, but it is perfectly fitted to your curves. Learn from Me, for I am gentle and humble of heart. *When you* are yoked to Me, your weary souls will find rest."

-Matthew 11:29

Read 1 John 1:8–9. What does humility begin with?

_____

Humility shows us Christ is the standard of righteousness. He's the One against whom we're to measure ourselves. Our goal should be to walk in the same righteousness in which He walked.

Consider the following statement:

Humility fosters unity, while pride fosters disunity.

How would pride among individuals foster disunity? Using a concordance, search the Scriptures, looking for verses that speak to pride, harmony, and humility. List them here.

_____

_____

_____

TWO: Humility produces gentleness.

In his commentary on Ephesians, John MacArthur says:

Many dictionaries define meekness in terms such as "timid," or "a deficiency in courage or spirit"; but that is far from the biblical meaning. *Praotēs* (here translated gentleness) refers to that which is mild-spirited and self-controlled, the opposite of vindictiveness and vengeance . . .

The meaning of *praotēs* has nothing to do with weakness, timidity, indifference, or cowardice. It was used of wild animals that were tamed, especially of horses that were broken and trained. Such an animal still has his strength and spirit, but its will is under the control of its master. The tamed lion is still powerful, but his power is under the control of his trainer. The horse can run just as fast, but he runs only when and where his master tells him to run.

Meekness is power under control. Biblical meekness, or gentleness, is power under the control of God. A meek person is normally quiet, soothing, and mild mannered, and he is never avenging, self-assertive, vindictive, or self-defensive.[1]

Read the following verses. What do they say about meekness or gentleness?

Matthew 5:5

_____

_____

Matthew 11:29

_____

_____

Galatians 5:22–23

_____

_____

Philippians 4:5

_____

_____

Colossians 3:12

_____

_____

THREE: Patience is a result of humility and gentleness.

The patient person accepts God's plan for everything and questions nothing.

Both *patience* and *longsuffering* come from the Greek word *makrothumia*, which means "a self-restraint of the mind before it gives room to action or passion; forbearance, long-suffering. The person who has power to avenge himself, yet refrains from the exercise of this power. It is patience with respect to persons. *Makrothumia* is associated with mercy and is used of God."[2]

It's the patient person who doesn't retaliate when he's wronged or hurt, but instead surrenders any anger and pain to God, allowing Him to replace that anger with patience and deal accordingly with the offender. God, who is rich in mercy, had great patience with us, His children—all the more reason why we should exercise patience with those in our lives.

Using a concordance, search the Scriptures, looking for verses that speak to patience, longsuffering, and/or God's mercy. List them here.

_____

_____

FOUR: Walking in the patience of God enables us to "tolerate one another in *an atmosphere thick with* love" (Ephesians 4:2).

Tolerance covers a multitude of sins, not for the purpose of ignoring or excusing those sins, but covering them such that they don't become any more of a flashing neon sign than necessary. As believers, we're called to help our brothers and sisters victoriously rise above their sin, not bring more attention to it.

> Above all, love each other deeply, because love covers over a multitude of sins.
>
> –1 Peter 4:8 (NIV)

Tolerant love is agape love. It's God-infused love, rooted and grounded in Christ, giving continually and unconditionally. Tolerant love expects nothing in return, giving selflessly and without reserve. Most importantly, tolerant love helps restore individuals to right standing with God.

Using a concordance, search the Scriptures, looking for verses and examples that speak of tolerant love.

_____

_____

_____

FIVE: Walking in humility, gentleness, patience, and tolerant love will preserve the unity the Spirit has already created, with peace binding us together.

How can the body be bound by peace?

_____

_____

Consider the following thought:

Spiritual **unity** is not, and cannot be, created by the church. It is already created by the Holy **Spirit**. "For by one Spirit we are all baptized into one body, whether Jews or Greeks, whether slaves or free, and we were all made to drink of one Spirit. . . . There are many members, but one body" (1 Corinthians 12:13, 20; cf. Romans 8:9).

The church's responsibility, through the lives of individual believers, is **to preserve the unity** by faithfully walking in a manner worthy of God's calling (v.1), manifesting Christ to the world by oneness in Him.[3]

Share your thoughts on spiritual unity in relation to the church's and the individual's responsibility in the promoting of this unity.

_____

_____

_____

_____

The basis of unity among believers is an overflow of the inward oneness we experience with God through the working of the Holy Spirit in our lives. We're one with others because we're one with the Spirit of the Lord. The two are inseparable.

e. (embrace)

Now that we've looked more into the characteristics of a worthy walk, let's go back and answer those questions that were posed earlier in today's lesson: Are you humble? Are you gentle? Are you patient? Does your love cover a multitude of sins, or expose them? Do you promote unity in the body? Spend some time with the Lord now, searching your heart. Ask Him to reveal those areas in your life that need to be infused with more of His character and love.

RECAPTURED CAPTIVES

Read Ephesians 4:4–6 . . .

Yes, the church is one body, united by all persons of the Godhead, but this unity doesn't cancel out the individual's responsibility to pick up his or her scalpel and move forward daily into deeper faith and relationship with Jesus.

Reread Ephesians 4:7. What do you think Paul means when he says, "*God* has given to each of us grace in full measure according to the Anointed's gift"?

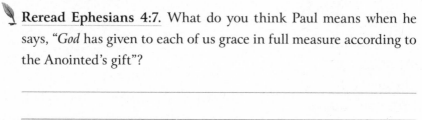

God's grace saves and enables the believer for service. At the moment of salvation, He gives to each of us a spiritual gift that's to be used to carry out the specific work He's fashioned us to accomplish.

🖋 **Read Romans 12:6–8; 1 Corinthians 12:8–10; and Ephesians 4:11 from the NKJV.** List all of the spiritual gifts that are mentioned in these passages.

_____

_____

_____

_____

🖋 At first glance, reading Ephesians 4:7 and then continuing on to Ephesians 4:8–10 from the NKJV, one might possibly wonder why Paul began this section of Scripture talking about gifts but now talks of "captivity captive" and "descend[ing] into the lower parts of the earth." Share your thoughts as to why you think Paul would do this.

> Each of you should use whatever gift you have received to serve others, as faithful stewards of God's grace in its various forms.
>
> -1 Peter 4:10 (NIV)

_____

_____

_____

_____

Paul is going to share with us some of the gifts God bestows upon His children, but before doing so he'll set the stage by explaining how Christ received the right to be the Giver of these gifts.

> Therefore He says:
> "When He ascended on high,
> He led captivity captive,
> And gave gifts to men."
> (Now this, "He ascended"-what does it
> mean but that He also first descended
> into the lower parts of the earth? He who
> descended is also the One who ascended
> far above all the heavens,
> that He might fill all things.)
> -Ephesians 4:8-10 (NKJV)

In this passage, Paul is quoting Psalm 68:18. Psalm 68 is a victory chant written by David in celebration of God's victory over the Jebusite city, the bringing back of the ark of the covenant (Israel's outward representation of God), and the triumphant ascent of the ark up to Mount Zion, the temple mount (2 Samuel 6–7; 1 Chronicles 13). Scholars believe Paul quotes this reference, not to say that it's an exact prediction of the coming Christ, but rather an analogy used to get across a point.

So what's the point? When a king conquered a city, he would bring back to his own city spoil, or treasures, from the enemy he'd captured. The king would parade these treasures and prisoners in the streets of his city for all to see. An Israelite king, in addition to parading the spoil and captives, would take his bounty up to Mount Zion. Proud of having freed his own people from the hands of the enemy, the king would publicly display the captives who'd been set free. These soldiers were often referred to as the *recaptured captives*. They were the captives who'd been captured by their own king, and because of their new captivity they were set free from the enemy.

In light of this explanation of Psalm 68:18, **read and break down Ephesians 4:8, and explain its meaning as you understand it.**

_____

_____

_____

_____

Captivity's captives are set free by the King who came to rescue them from the bondage of the enemy. Oh, how I have been bound by the enemy! Chained by pride, jealousy, envy. Bound tightly by lies that I was nothing, useless, of no value. Burdened with shame and guilt. Unable to lift my head. A slave to the one who desired to bleed my life dry.

But King Jesus came! He came from His throne on high. He broke my chains. He replaced the captor's lies with His magnificent truth. He lifted my burden and He gave me new life. He captured me and made me His own. And now, He parades me as His child, His precious treasure, one whom He dearly loves.

My friend, the battle has been won! King Jesus came just as much for you as He did for me. His defeat of the enemy was for you. He means for you to live in His victory. He means to capture you and make you His very own special treasure! He means for you to be a recaptured captive!

Read Ephesians 4:9 from the NKJV. Who ascended? When did He ascend? What does it mean that "He also first descended into the lower parts of the earth"? Use Scripture to support your answer.

_____

_____

_____

We talk often of Christ's ascension to heaven after God raised Him from the grave, but we must never forget the fact that He also descended. He descended from heaven to earth, taking on human flesh to walk among a people who desperately needed Him. Christ, the Redeemer, descended into the depths of Sheol, the abode of the dead, to proclaim His victory over death, hell, and the grave so that we could have new life in Him.

Read Ephesians 4:10 from the NKJV. What do you think Paul means when he says, "that He might fill all things"?

_____

_____

_____

Read Philippians 2:9–11. How was Christ honored once He ascended to heaven after His work on earth was done?

_____

_____

_____

Now back to the question asked at the beginning of today's lesson. Why does Paul begin talking about gifts in Ephesians 4:7 and then talk of "captivity captive" and "descend[ing] into the lower parts of the earth" in Ephesians 4:8–10?

_____

_____

_____

Paul's point here is this: Jesus descending from heaven to earth and suffering death to redeem lost mankind qualified Him to be exalted far above the heavens to the throne of God. Because of His glorious victory over death, He now has the right to rule His church and bestow gifts upon His children as He sees fit.

King Jesus is the only One qualified to be the Gift Giver.

EQUIPPING AND BUILDING

 Read Ephesians 4:11. List the gifts Christ has the authority to give those whom He calls into service for Him.

_____

_____

_____

d. (define)

Using a *Strong's Concordance* or Bible dictionary, define the following spiritually gifted leaders as listed in the New King James Version's rendering of verse 11.

Apostle

_____

_____

Prophet

_____

_____

_____

> See
> Appendix I
> for FREE
> online tools
> that contain
> a *Strong's*
> *Concordance.*

Evangelist

_____

_____

Pastor and teacher

_____

_____

Read Ephesians 4:12–16. What investigative questions can you ask of these verses? For what purpose are spiritual gifts given?

_____

_____

_____

A believer's job is to use his or her gifts to bring about unity in the body and to lead others to an intimate knowledge of God. You and I are to be pouring into the lives of others what God has taught us. The kicker here is this: We can't pour out what we aren't being filled up with. But as we sit at the feet of Jesus and feast on His Word, we're filled to overflowing. Then we can—and should—go forth, spilling out Jesus' love on others. How we spill out His Word and truth is our gift.

Read Ephesians 4:14. What is the result of a believer using his or her gifts to serve the body?

_____

_____

_____

A believer who serves the body of Christ with his or her gifts equips other believers with sound doctrine so those younger in the faith are growing up and becoming mature in God. If believers aren't utilizing the gifts Christ has given them to serve the body, immature believers will be easily persuaded by false truths and teachings.

Read Ephesians 4:15–16:

> By truth spoken in love, we are to grow in every way into Him—the Anointed One, the head. He joins and holds together the whole body with its ligaments providing the support needed so each part works to its proper design to form a healthy, *growing, and mature* body that builds itself up in love.

In using our gifts to serve others, how are we to teach and minister?

_____

What do you think Paul means when he says, "Grow in every way into Him—the Anointed One, the head"?

_____

_____

_____

In all areas of our lives, we're to be growing to be more like Christ. And in love, we're to be teaching and leading others to do the same. To grow in Christlikeness is to be completely subjected to His control and obedient to His will. It means that one is surrendered totally to God's plan in his or her life no matter the end result of that mission.

 Who is the head of the body?

Christ is the head of the body. He is the unifier of the body. And He is the source of life, power, and strength for His body, the church. He puts the body together as He sees fit, giving each member a specific purpose.

The church grows, flourishes, and is able to carry out its mission when all its members are submitting to God, loving one another unconditionally and working together as a united force.

 ## e. (embrace)

Are you spending purposeful time in the Word and in conversation with God, cultivating intimacy with Him so that you're able to pour into the lives of others? Are you using your gifts to serve the body? Are you humbling yourself before God and your fellow brothers and sisters in Christ? Do you love others with a pure love, speaking God's truth with compassion and mercy? Are you united as one with the body God has placed you in?

We've talked a lot about spiritual gifts in this lesson. Maybe you're wondering what gifts the Lord has given you. I'd like to encourage you to do a few things today:

1. Pray. Ask God to show you how He's gifted you.

2. Complete a spiritual gifts assessment. Ask your pastor or women's ministry leader if there's a particular gifts assessment he or she recommends. If not, I recommend the Gifted2Serve Spiritual Gifts Inventory from BuildingChurch.net. (http://buildingchurch.net/g2s-i.htm). I do want to caution you before you take any type of assessment: these assessments aren't a be-all and

end-all in determining your spiritual gifts, but they will shed light on your natural bent and how God has wired you.

3. Start using your gifts to edify and strengthen the body. Once you become clearer on what your gifts are, begin cultivating growth in those areas of giftedness. Seek out opportunities in your church and community to use the gifts God has given you.

PAUSED APPLAUSE

In this lesson, we've also talked a lot about unity. Being one. Benefiting the body of Christ. These are all themes of Paul's writings thus far in Ephesians 4. I can't help but wonder as I think back over these verses, Is the body of Christ unified? Are we working together as one united force sharing Jesus with those dead in trespasses and sins? Are we serving our brothers and sisters in Christ, encouraging them to continue growing in their relationship with the Lord?

I've seen some very ugly sides of the body of Christ: backstabbing, gossip, sabotage, comparison of one's gifts and calling to another's. In fact, I've been tangled up in it myself.

★ ★ ★

They sit on the stage together, a young married couple, the pastor to their left. Their children, one girl and one boy, are little. In a few short months they'll make their home in a different land, surrounded by a different people group, learning and speaking a different language. They tell their story: how they've sold worldly possessions, given away treasures, rid themselves of the "American dream" and said yes to their "Jesus calling."

I sit and listen, nodding and smiling and even wiping away tears as they share how God has paved this way for them. They ask for support and prayers, and corporately we, the church, agree to lift prayers to the throne for their family, for their mission, for their Jesus calling.

Their time of sharing concludes, and we pray and applaud their "yes." But then, my applause of support and encouragement pauses. And I drop my hands onto my lap and wonder, *Am I doing enough for Jesus? Am I saying yes to my Jesus calling?*

He stands, the preacher's son, beside his dad, the preacher. And this preacher-dad tells us how proud he is of his son. He tells us of the years of wilderness roaming his son experienced and of the place to which God has now brought him. I sit up straighter in my seat. My eyes spill over with tears. I've lived this preacher's son's story: the preacher's daughter who chose her own way, who spent many years wandering through wilderness lands.

This redeemed wilderness traveler spent some time in a foreign land, and now he's going to do it again, he tells us . . . this time for Jesus. For eleven months he'll make his home in eleven different lands, ministering to different people groups, learning and speaking different languages.

Their time of sharing concludes and we pray for this preacher's son, we commission him, and we applaud his "yes." But again, my applause of support and encouragement pauses. And I drop my hands onto my lap and wonder, *Am I doing enough for Jesus? Am I saying yes to my Jesus calling?*

I flip through the mail and stop when I see her smiling face. She has sent us a prayer postcard. She's traveling to a different land this summer, to minister to a people group different from her own, and she'll learn to speak a different language in order to tell others of Jesus' love. My heart swells with pride. She's not my own, but I'm so very proud of the Jesus-loving young lady she's becoming. She's saying yes to her Jesus calling, pursuing Him on this trip, seeking out His plans for her life.

I place her prayer postcard in my Bible so I'll remember to pray for her daily. And this is what I pray for: wisdom for God's leading into this ripe field of missions, boldness to speak truth to those He places in her path, a compassionate heart to meet the hurting in their pain, willing hands to serve those in need, the eyes of Jesus to see into the lives of those who live in darkness, ears to hear words not spoken, tenderness to know the Spirit's leading, and, above all, an obedient heart to follow hard after Jesus.

I send her an e-mail, telling her how excited I am for her and how I have no doubt God has great plans for her life. I encourage her to continue to seek God's face in all things. I tell her I love her, I thank her for the privilege to pray for her, and I applaud her "yes."

But once more, my applause of support and encouragement pauses. And I drop my hands onto my lap, where my Bible sits open, a prayer postcard staring up at me, and I wonder, *Am I doing enough for Jesus? Am I saying yes to my Jesus calling?*

I listen to all these stories and many others: stories of those adopting, of people digging wells for the thirsty, of others organizing food drives for the hungry, and of still others nursing the sick. I applaud them all; really I do. But every time, I drop my hands and I wonder, *Am I doing enough for Jesus? Am I saying yes to my Jesus calling?*

Maybe I'm the only one who looks at others and thinks that my doing isn't enough. Maybe . . . but I doubt it. I think we all suffer from paused applause, handclaps of praise ceased in midair because we suddenly wonder if we're doing enough for Jesus and fulfilling His calling.

What I've come to understand and embrace is this: God has created us all uniquely different and called us each to a different "yes." And He's asking each of us to drop our hands, not in paused applause, but in total surrender, to do whatever, wherever, and however. To live a surrendered "yes" life that results in our being a catalyst to others stepping forward from the shallows into deeper faith and relationship with Jesus. Our yeses aren't the same; they can't be compared. My Jesus "yes" can only be lived out to its fullest by me, no one else. And the same goes for you; only you can live out your Jesus "yes."

So, am I doing enough for Jesus? Are you doing enough for Jesus? If we're dropping our hands in surrender, saying yes to our Jesus callings—whether that "yes" is . . .

- doing (again) the same Monday morning mountain of laundry;
- washing a sink full of dirty dishes;
- changing dirty diapers and wiping runny noses;
- loving on and encouraging a woman who just lost her spouse;
- counseling and strengthening the couple who want to end their marriage;
- preparing dinner for a family agonizing over a wayward child;
- listening to a recovering addict tell his or her story;
- chatting and laughing with a lesbian or gay friend over coffee; or
- spending a Saturday at the homeless shelter, playing card games with the residents—

whatever our "yes" is, then we're absolutely doing enough for Jesus, and our applause for others should never pause because we're all fulfilling our kingdom purpose.

d.i.v.e. into LESSON TWO

d. (define)

i. (investigate)

v. (visualize)

e. (embrace)

Off with the Old, on with the New

Ephesians 4:17-24

 Before you begin your time of study and learning, spend a few moments in prayer asking God to give you an open heart and mind to learn new truths from His Word.

 ### v. (visualize)

Take a snapshot of Ephesians 4 by reading through the chapter at least three times, reminding yourself of the big picture. Review your WOW from chapter 4. Don't forget to add to your outline/paraphrase.

In this lesson we're going to zoom in on Ephesians 4:17–24. As you read these verses again, begin to d.i.v.e. below the surface.

CHARACTERISTICS OF AN UNGODLY WALK

 Read Ephesians 4:17–19.

A call to salvation is a call to newness of life. It's a call to a new kind of walking.

In verses 17–19, Paul gives us four characteristics of the ungodly way that believers are no longer to walk in. List those characteristics below.

1._____

2._____

3._____

4._____

ONE: "futility of their mind, having their understanding darkened" (v. 17–18 NKJV)

d. (define)

Define *futility* as found in Ephesians 4:17 (NKJV).

_____

_____

The person without the Spirit does not accept the things that come from the Spirit of God but considers them foolishness, and cannot understand them because they are discerned only through the Spirit.

-1 Corinthians 2:14 (NIV)

Any ungodly, unregenerate, pagan person walks in a manner that is devoid of truth. He lives his life and conducts himself in opposition to the things of God because he doesn't understand the ways of God.

Read Romans 1:21–28. What do these verses say about the life of the ungodly?

_____

_____

_____

_____

_____

As those who belong to the body of Christ, believers are to conduct themselves in submission to God and His standards of living.

Read 1 John 2:6 and write it here.

_____

_____

TWO: "strangers and aliens to the kind of life God has for them" (Ephesians 4:18)

The ungodly walk in such a manner that it shows they're separated from God. **Read Isaiah 44:9–20 (focus on verses 18–20).** What do these verses say about those who are alienated from God?

_____

_____

_____

_____

_____

_____

Consider Strong's definition of "blindness" as found in Ephesians 4:18 (NKJV).

pórósis—stupidity or *callousness:* —blindness, hardness[1]

The cause of the ungodly person's darkness and/or alienation from Christ and his lack of understanding of the things of God is the hardness and callousness of his heart. Because humankind rejects God, God determines to give them over to the lusts of their flesh.

So God gave them just what their lustful hearts desired. *As a result,* they violated their bodies and invited shame into their lives.

-Romans 1:24

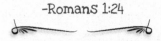

THREE: "lost all natural feelings" (Ephesians 4:19)

The ungodly become numb to their sin. The more they sin, the more their hearts become emotionless. The effects of their sin mean nothing to them. And as sin continues to increase, a sense of complete apathy takes over their lives. Not only do their godless choices affect them, but the consequences of these choices begin to affect others as well.

Despite the fact that they are fully aware that God's law says this way of life deserves death, they fail to stop. And *worse*-they applaud others on this destructive path.

-Romans 1:32

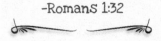

FOUR: "have given themselves over to sensual, greedy, and reckless living. They stop at nothing to satisfy their impure appetites." (Ephesians 4:19)

No longer holding to any kind of moral standards or restraints, the ungodly have become all about their selfish desires.

For you have spent enough time in the past doing what pagans choose to do—living in debauchery, lust, drunkenness, orgies, carousing and detestable idolatry.

-1 Peter 4:3 (NIV)

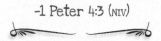

The life of the ungodly is characterized by a desire to please self. "But," Paul says in Ephesians 4:20, "you have not so learned Christ" but "have been taught by Him" (v. 20–21 NKJV).

 What does it mean to "learn Christ" and to be "taught by Him"?

_____

_____

To learn Christ is to have a personal relationship with Him. This fellowship is based on the Word of God (John 5:39). The believer has learned Christ through His death, burial, and resurrection. And because we've learned Him and have been taught by Him, we're to get rid of our former way of living.

 ## SAYING GOOD-BYE TO THE OLD LIFE

 ### d. (define)

Read Ephesians 4:22. Using a *Strong's Concordance*, define the term *put off* as found in the New King James Version.

_____

_____

Based on this definition, what are some practical ways you can "put off" behaviors from your ungodly past?

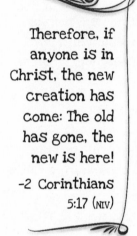

Therefore, if anyone is in Christ, the new creation has come: The old has gone, the new is here!

-2 Corinthians 5:17 (NIV)

_____

_____

_____

_____

_____

As we "put off" the old self, we're to "put on" the newness of Christ and we're to be renewed in the spirit of our minds. Because of our new citizenship, the desires and ideas of our past life without Christ should no longer control us.

As new creations in Christ, we're to put on and live as the person God created us to be, reflecting His character of righteousness and holiness.

 e. (embrace)

How can we renew our minds? How can we get rid of false beliefs, ideas, and that irrational thinking that can so easily control our thought patterns, which, in turn, affect our behavior?

Read John 17:17; Romans 12:1–2; and Philippians 4:8. Write down other verses (use the cross-references the verses in John, Romans, and Philippians lead you to) that speak to controlling your thoughts and renewing your mind. Begin forming a plan that will help you to daily renew your mind so your thinking lines up with the truths found in God's Word. (See Appendix V for Scriptures to implant to help you in your daily walk.)

_____

_____

_____

_____

_____

_____

Finally, brothers and sisters, fill your minds with *beauty and* truth. Meditate on whatever is honorable, whatever is right, whatever is pure, whatever is lovely, whatever is good, whatever is virtuous and praiseworthy.

-Philippians 4:8

d.i.v.e. into LESSON THREE

d. (define)

i. (investigate)

v. (visualize)

e. (embrace)

Standards for New Living

Ephesians 4:25-5:2

 Before you begin your time of study and learning, spend a few moments in prayer asking God to give you an open heart and mind to learn new truths from His Word.

 ## v. (visualize)

Take a snapshot of Ephesians 4 by reading through the chapter at least three times, reminding yourself of the big picture. Review your WOW from chapter 4. Don't forget to add to your outline/paraphrase.

In this lesson we're going to zoom in on Ephesians 4:25–5:2. As you read these verses again, begin to d.i.v.e. below the surface.

HERE'S WHAT YOU'RE TO DO

 Read Ephesians 4:25–32. In these closing verses, Paul shares with us specific ungodly behaviors that believers are to put off and the godly behaviors they're to put on.

It's time for another solo d.i.v.e. You did it earlier on in our study, and I'm confident you can do it again! Using the d.i.v.e. method, carefully go through these eight verses. Make lists, define words, use cross references, ask investigative questions, visualize and paraphrase the text, and embrace God's challenge to you. Study the words God breathed through the apostle Paul. You can do it!

I'll help you get started with the framework . . .

Ephesians 4:25: The new man is to put off lying and put on truth.

_____

_____

_____

Ephesians 4:26: The new man is to put off unrighteous anger and put on righteous anger.

_____

_____

_____

Ephesians 4:28: The new man is to put off stealing and put on honest work and sharing.

_____

_____

_____

Ephesians 4:29: The new man is to put off unwholesome talk and put on words of encouragement.

_____

_____

_____

Ephesians 4:30: The new man is to put off natural vices and put on spiritual virtues.

_____

_____

_____

Walking worthy of the calling to which we've been called isn't an easy task, but it isn't impossible either. It involves a putting off of our old way of living and replacing it with the newness of Christ Jesus.

e. (embrace)

What in your life do you need to put off, to lay aside, to get rid of? Are you easily angered? Do you hold grudges? Is there someone in your life you need to forgive? Do you need to seek forgiveness from somone? Are you humble? gentle? patient? Does your love cover a multitude of sins or expose them? Do you promote unity in the body?

It could be that, as you read through these questions, other thoughts, actions, or behaviors come to mind. Spend a few moments processing through these thoughts. Take time to answer these questions honestly, and then formulate an action plan that will help you put off the old and put on the newness of Jesus.

_____

_____

_____

_____

_____

_____

ATTRIBUTES BELIEVERS ARE TO IMITATE

Read the following passages and write them in the spaces provided.

Ephesians 4:1:

_____

_____

Ephesians 4:17:

_____

_____

Ephesians 5:2:

_____

_____

Read Ephesians 5:1–2.

d. (define)

Using a *Strong's Concordance*, define the term *imitators* as found in Ephesians 5:1 and the term *walk* as found in Ephesians 5:2 (NKJV).

_____

_____

As believers in Christ, walking in love is an outward expression of the inward transformation that's taken place in our hearts; it's an overflowing response of what God has done for us. Daily we're to become more and more like Him, mimicking His attributes of kindness, compassion, tenderness, humility, and servitude.

Using a concordance, search the Scriptures for other attributes of God that we're to imitate. Write those verses in the spaces provided. I'll help you get started.

Matthew 5:48:

_____

_____

_____

_____

1 Peter 1:15–16:

_____

_____

_____

_____

> He knew those who would be His one day, and He chose them beforehand to be conformed to the image of His Son so that Jesus would be the firstborn of a new family of believers, all brothers and sisters.
>
> -Romans 8:29

WALKING IN GOD'S LOVE

One of the many characteristics of God we're to imitate is His love. Not only are we to be "rooted and grounded in love," Paul says we're also to *walk in* this love (Ephesians 5:2 NKJV). What would you say is the greatest evidence of love? Why?

_____

_____

_____

_____

There are many evidences of love, but quite possibly one of the greatest evidences of one's love for another is forgiveness—more specifically, an undeserved forgiveness.

Read the following verses and write them in the spaces provided.

Ephesians 1:7:

_____

_____

_____

Ephesians 4:32:

_____

_____

_____

Colossians 2:13:

_____

_____

_____

According to these three verses, what was/is evidence of God's love for us?

_____

_____

_____

Our capacity to love, and in turn forgive others, is based on our understanding of how much God has forgiven us.

Christ forgave out of His abundant love for us. His forgiveness was something that we in no way deserved. He forgave expecting nothing in return. He forgave sacrificially. And He forgave completely.

As imitators of God, we should forgive as He forgives: in love, with no conditions, expecting nothing in return, completely and without reserve.

 e. (embrace)

Unforgiveness is the measure of self-righteousness just as forgiveness is the measure of love.[1]

-John MacArthur

Christ's agape love is evidenced by His forgiveness, and that forgiveness is evidenced by His giving of Himself freely as an offering and sacrifice to make atonement for us. Through Christ, God displayed to those whom He foreknew an unconditional, undeserved love.

But God showed
his great love for
us by sending
Christ to die for
us while we were
still sinners.

-Romans 5:8 (NLT)

For since our friendship
with God was restored by
the death of his Son while
we were still his enemies,
we will certainly be saved
through the life of his Son.

-Romans 5:10 (NLT)

<u>Reread Ephesians 5:1–2.</u>

Christ's offering and sacrifice was a sweet-smelling aroma to God, an aroma of victory.

THE FRAGRANT AROMA OF OFFERINGS

i. (investigate)

Read Leviticus 1–5. What five offerings does God command the Israelites to partake in? What is the purpose for each? What do each of these offerings represent in relation to Christ? In relation to Christ, do all of these offerings please God? Why or why not?

1._____

_____

_____

2._____

_____

_____

3._____

_____

_____

4._____

_____

_____

5._____

_____

_____

The Burnt Offering	Leviticus 1:1–17	This offering represented Christ's complete devotion to God in the giving of His life in obedience.
The Grain Offering	Leviticus 2:1–16	This offering represented Christ's perfection.
The Peace Offering	Leviticus 3:1–17; 4:27–31	This offering represented Christ's making peace between God and man.
The Sin Offering	Leviticus 4:1–26, 32–35	This offering represented Christ's substitutionary death and atonement for our sins.
The Guilt Offering	Leviticus 5:1–19	This offering represented Christ's payment for our redemption.

Reread Leviticus 1:9, 13, 17; 2:2, 9; 3:5, 16.

The burnt offering, grain offering, and peace offering provided "a sweet aroma" (NKJV) to the Lord.

As Christ hung on the cross, He was the sin offering and the guilt offering for us. God turned His back on His Son because in that very moment Christ became our sin—sin that a holy God could not look upon nor be pleased with.

For God made Christ, who never sinned, to be
the offering for our sin, so that we could be
made right with God through Christ.

-2 Corinthians 5:21 (NLT)

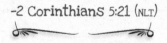

When Christ was raised from the dead, conquering sin and the grave, God was pleased and Christ's selfless, sacrificial gift of love and forgiveness were a fragrant aroma to the Father, the very scent of victory.

Read 2 Corinthians 2:14–16 from *The Message*:

> In the Messiah, in Christ, God leads us from place to place in one perpetual victory parade. Through us, he brings knowledge of Christ. Everywhere we go, people breathe in the exquisite fragrance. Because of Christ, we give off a sweet scent rising to God, which is recognized by those on the way of salvation—an aroma redolent with life. But those on the way to destruction treat us more like the stench from a rotting corpse.

e. (embrace)

Are you giving off an aroma of victory or the stench of death? As children of God, we're to carry this aroma of victory with us everywhere we go.

Let's do a little scratch-n-sniff test? Scratch below your exterior and peer into your heart. What does your scratch-n-sniff test reveal? Are you giving off the sweet smelling aroma of victory or the stinky stench of death? Where do you land on the scratch-n-sniff scale? If you find yourself landing more toward the stinky side, jot down a few action steps you can take that will begin leading you toward the sweet. And even if you find yourself to be on the sweeter end of things, there's always room for improvement, right? So, jot down a few action steps you can take in order to continue cultivating sweetness in your life.

●━━━━━━━━━━━━━━━━━━━━━━━━━●

Sweet   Stinky

_____

_____

Monkey See, Monkey Do

EPHESIANS FIVE

d.i.v.e. into LESSON ONE

d. (define)

i. (investigate)

v. (visualize)

e. (embrace)

LESSON ONE

Have NO Part In . . .

Ephesians 5:3-14

 Before you begin your time of study and learning, spend a few moments in prayer asking God to give you an open heart and mind to learn new truths from His Word.

 ### v. (visualize)

Take a snapshot of Ephesians 5 by reading through the chapter at least three times, reminding yourself of the big picture. As you're reading, make note of any verse(s) that tugs at your heart; this may be the WOW God is giving you to embrace from chapter 5. Begin to develop your own outline/paraphrase.

In this lesson we're going to zoom in on Ephesians 5:3–14. As you read these verses again, begin to d.i.v.e. below the surface.

 ## HAVE NO PART IN

Paul tells believers in Ephesians 5:1–2 to be imitators of God, walk in love, and exude a sweet-smelling aroma everywhere they go. In verses 3–7, he tells them how they're *not* to behave.

Dive Deeper

🖋 **Read Ephesians 5:3–7.** List below the behaviors Paul says a believer is to have no part in.

_____

_____

_____

_____

Notice from your list that anything God creates, Satan seeks to destroy. God forgives, loves with a pure love, is selfless, and willingly sacrifices for the benefit of others. Satan is a polar opposite. He accuses, he doesn't have the ability to love, and he's only out to benefit himself.

Consider Thayer's Greek Definitions for the following terms as found in Ephesians 5:3 (NKJV).[1]

Fornication—*porneia*: illicit sexual intercourse;

    1a) adultery, fornication, homosexuality, lesbianism, intercourse with animals, etc.

    1b) sexual intercourse with close relatives; Lev. 18

    1c) sexual intercourse with a divorced man or woman

    2) metaphorically, the worship of idols

Uncleanness—*akatharsia*

    1) uncleanness

    1a) physical

    1b) in a moral sense: the impurity of lustful, luxurious, profligate living

    1b1) of impure motives

Covetousness—*pleonexia*

greedy desire to have more, covetousness, avarice

God created sex. He created it to be a beautiful expression of love between a husband and his wife. He intended this union to be enjoyable, pleasurable, and honoring of each person. Our sexual nature is a gift from God, a gift meant to be adored and cherished and treasured for a lifetime. But Satan has taken God's gift, untied the bow, torn off the wrapping, dumped the treasure on the ground, and stomped it, leaving it broken into a million pieces.

Herein lies the problem with sex: Satan has tricked us into equating sex with an emotional high of feeling "loved" when in actuality it is only lust masked. This false persona of love is selfish and lethal. It's conditional, founded on what it can get or take from another. Its stay is temporary yet its effects are eternal. It seeks only to be gratified and doesn't desire to serve . . . all because lust masked is not love rooted and grounded in Christ.

Lust masked lures unsuspecting victims into its lairs and drains them of all sense of worth. I know this because by the time I was sixteen, I'd been deceived by false personas of love, lured into the self-centered worlds of others, and stripped of every ounce of self-worth I had. Then, from my own pain and shattered world, I did to others what had been done to me. Out of selfishness and a desire to avenge what had been taken from me, I manipulated, deceived, beat down, and sabotaged anyone who attempted to get close to me. And I did it all masked as a Jesus follower.

Only through Jesus have I been able to overcome and heal, forgive and seek forgiveness. But the price has been huge and the scars remain.

Every time I turn on the news, I hear a headline story about sexual abuse, molestation, rape, pornography, prostitution, or sex trafficking. The statistics of those fallen prey to the selfishness and lustful desires of others are staggering and sickening.

My state, North Carolina, ranks in the top ten on the FBI's list of states most likely to have trafficking occur, because of the highways, the large military bases, and its location as a coastal state.[2] Over the past year I've personally become involved with a local organization, Transforming Hope Ministries, that provides safety, counsels, and helps reacclimatize girls who've been victims of sex trafficking. It's one way I can share my story of sexual abuse and healing with a heart that's hurting, one way I pray God is able to use my pain for His ultimate glory.

Human trafficking is a form of modern-day slavery. Victims of human trafficking are subjected to force, fraud, or coercion for the purpose of commercial sex, debt bondage, or forced labor. They are young children, teenagers, men and women. The US Trafficking Victims Protection Act of 2000 defines *sex trafficking* as the recruitment, harboring, transportation, provision, or obtaining of a person for the purpose of a commercial sex act where such an act is induced by force, fraud, or coercion, or in which the person has not attained 18 years of age or for the purpose of labor through involuntary servitude, peonage, debt bondage, or slavery.[3]

 e. (embrace)

If you've been the target of another's apathy and disregard for his or her sexual behavior or if you've been the one manipulating and hurting others, please know God is in the business of healing and restoring. Lay your hurt and those wounds at His feet. Allow Him to work a miraculous healing in your life. You're meant to live in freedom, not chained to pain and brokenness.

Whether or not you've personally been a victim of sexual abuse, there are girls and boys, women and men who need your help. You can get involved and help those who've been victims of sexual sins turn life as they know it into something beautiful. We can make a difference!

SPEAK THANKS

Paul says such sins as fornication, uncleanness, and covetousness should not even be named among believers. Not only should there be no form or hint of sexual immorality; there should also be no hint of filthiness, foolish talking, or coarse jesting.

 ### d. (define)

Using a *Strong's Concordance*, define the following terms as found in Ephesians 5:4 in the New King James Version.

filthiness

_____

_____

foolish talking

_____

_____

coarse jesting

_____

_____

God's standards are clear—there should be NO filthiness, foolish talking, or coarse jesting coming from the mouth of the one who follows after Him. Instead, believers should always be speaking praise and be known for their spirit and attitude of unending thankfulness.

Give thanks *to God* no matter what circumstances
you find yourself in. (This is God's will for
all of you in Jesus the Anointed.)

-1 Thessalonians 5:18

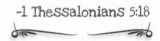

Thankfulness comes from a selfless heart. Whatever good a thankful person receives, he knows it comes from God and is something he doesn't, in reality, deserve to receive.

Quickly list a handful of things you're thankful for. Stop right now and thank God for those things and/or people He's blessed you with.

_____

_____

_____

_____

_____

Read Ephesians 5:5:

This is what we know for certain: no one who engages in loose sex, impure actions, and greed—which is just a form of idolatry—has any inheritance in the kingdom of God and His Anointed.

Why does Paul say no person who is involved in habitual sin will inherit the kingdom of God?

_____

_____

A lifestyle of habitual sin consists of behavior that goes against the Word of God. Romans 6; 2 Corinthians 5:17; and 1 John teach about the new nature of the one who belongs to God's kingdom. God's children have in them the very person of God and carry with them His nature of holiness. Someone involved in habitual sin attests that he doesn't belong to God.

Everyone who has been born into God's family avoids sin as a *lifestyle* because the genes of God's children come from God Himself. Therefore, a child of God can't live a life of persistent sin. So it is not hard to figure out who are the children of God and who are the children of the diabolical one: those who lack right standing and those who don't show love for one another do not belong to God.

-1 John 3:9-10

We have cause to celebrate because the grace of God has appeared, offering *the gift of* salvation to all people. *Grace arrives* with its own instruction: run away from anything that leads us away from God; abandon the lusts and passions of this world; live life now in this age *with awareness* and self-control, doing the right thing and keeping yourselves holy.

-Titus 2:11-12

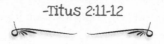

A WARNING

Paul closes this section of Scripture with the following warning . . .

Don't be fooled by people whose sentences are compounded with *useless words,* empty words—*they just show they are empty souls.* For, in His wrath, God will judge all the children of disobedience for these kinds *of sins.* So don't *be persuaded into their ignorance;* and *don't* cast your lot with them.

-Ephesians 5:6-7

Believers are warned not to be deceived by those who teach that sin is tolerable and God will accept all into His kingdom. Empty words that tickle the ears and aid in rationalizing one's sins are void of truth and cause a person to travel farther into lifestyles of sin instead of encouraging him or her to repent and turn from those sins.

According to Ephesians 5:6, what will happen to those who disobey God?

_____

Christians aren't sinless nor are they perfect. But it's a dangerous thing for them to allow professing believers to continue living in habitual sin. The body of Christ cannot and should not agree with professing believers who are living lifestyles of habitual sin, and who assume that all is right with them and God. A heart that truly belongs to God should feel conviction over sin and desire to be brought back into right relationship with the Father.

WALKING IN GOD'S LIGHT

As imitators of Christ, we're to walk in love. Paul showed us examples of both real and counterfeit love in the first seven verses of Ephesians 5. In verses 8–14, he's going to focus on imitating God in relation to light.

Read Ephesians 5:8–14.

 What do you think Paul means when he says, "Although you were once the personification of darkness, you are now light in the Lord" in verse 8?

_____

_____

We learned from Ephesians 2 that darkness is the state or point at which people are dead in trespasses and sin, devoid of truth, and spiritually separated from God. We also learned these individuals are ruled by the power of the darkness, which is Satan.

In Scripture, light and darkness are very common metaphors. Intellectually, light refers to Biblical truth and knowledge, while darkness refers to dishonesty and foolishness. Morally, light refers to holiness and purity while darkness refers to sin or wrongdoing.

Light represents Christ in His truth, wisdom, holiness, and perfection. Darkness represents Satan and all of his demonic forces in their lies, schemes, rebellion, evilness, and ignorance.

Keeping in mind that the book of Ephesians is written to believers, note that Paul says to those believers, "You once lived a life that was devoid of truth. You were once separated spiritually from God, unable to enjoy any kind of fellowship with Him. Your life was ruled by Satan. But now you are light in the Lord; you are light because God is light." He encourages us to walk in the light, for it is the Light who rescued every believer, bestowing salvation through His

blood upon each one. As we walk in light and pattern our lives after the truths set before us in Scripture, God's plan for our lives will become clear. We'll see with enlightened spiritual eyes what's right and what's acceptable in the sight of God.

But you are a chosen people, *set aside to be* a royal order of priests, a holy nation, God's own; so that you may proclaim the wondrous acts of the One who called you out of *inky* darkness into shimmering light.

-1 Peter 2:9

The Eternal is my light amidst *my darkness* and my rescue *in times of trouble.* So whom shall I fear? He surrounds me with a fortress of protection. So nothing should cause me alarm.

-Psalm 27:1

HOLDING ONE ANOTHER ACCOUNTABLE

Read Ephesians 5:11–13 and Galatians 6:1–3. According to these passages, what are Christians to do if a brother or sister in Christ is living in sin?

_____

_____

_____

_____

One of the Christian's responsibilities in belonging to the body of Christ is to hold other believers accountable in behavior and lifestyle. Scripture clearly teaches that we're to confront sin in the lives of our brothers and sisters for the purpose of leading them to repentance and restoration.

We're also to hold everything up to the light of truth in order to expose the evil within and seek the good. In confronting another's sin we must be sure that we act in love and not condemnation. We must confront for the purpose of healing, not further destruction.

Because we are one in the body of Christ and are walking this journey on earth together, we must spur one another on to live godly lives that reflect the character of the one and only God who dwells within our spirits.

 ## e. (embrace)

Are you open to a sister in Christ confronting you should she see sin hindering you in growing your relationship with God? Do you have an accountability sister or small group in your life that can keep you in check? If not, ask God to send individuals into your life who will speak the truth of God's Word over you and into you. Also, ask God to make your heart receptive to the counsel of others.

 # AN INVITATION

Read Ephesians 5:14. In this verse Paul extends an invitation to those who are walking in darkness to enter into the light of the holiness of God. It's a call from lostness to salvation.

In the spaces provided, break down the call to salvation as found in Ephesians 5:14 in the New King James Version.

"Therefore He says . . ."

Who is speaking?

_____

"Awake, you who sleep."

Who is he addressing?

"Arise from the dead."

What is this a call to?

"And Christ will give you light."

What does this promise and from whom will it come?

"You are like that illuminating light. Let your light shine everywhere you go, *that you may illumine creation,* so men and women everywhere may see your good actions, may see creation at its fullest, may see your devotion to Me, and may turn and praise your Father in heaven because of it."

–Matthew 5:16

God calls sinners who sleep to repentance and promises them redemption through His Son, Jesus Christ.

Every man and woman has been or is right now spiritually dead because of his or her sin. The spiritually dead live life asleep to the things of God. It is only the shining light of Christ that wakes us and lights our path, enabling and equipping us to walk worthy of the calling to which we have been called.

When we're awakened by the light of Christ, it's then our job to allow His light to shine through us so others see His glory. As Christians, we're to carry His light in this dark world. Being a flaming torch for Christ is both a privilege and a great responsibility. Each of us is called to be a city on a hill that's not to be hidden, but is instead to boldly proclaim Jesus as the light of the world come to put to sleep forever the sins that entangle.

For once you were full of darkness, but now you have light from the Lord. So live as people of light!

—Ephesians 5:8 (NLT)

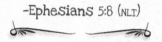

THERE IS A KING AT BURGER KING

It was Thursday morning, our scheduled weekly play date with friends. On this particular day, we five mamas and our herd of young'uns met at Burger King because it was deathly hot outside, and who in the world wants to sweat when there's AC?

I saw her as we walked into the playroom. She sat, head down, alone in the corner. On the tray in front of her were two small drinks, a few fries, a balled-up hamburger wrapper, and a blob of leftover ketchup.

As my kids began climbing the play equipment, I noticed a lone little boy, probably five years old, running through the overhead tunnels. *He must be her baby*, I thought. Sure enough, every so often he'd run up to the table where his mama sat, take a sip of drink, pat her on the shoulder, then run back to play.

Their interactions were strangely odd yet extremely fascinating. And so I watched from my table on the opposite side of the playroom. My friends chatted and laughed and reminded our herd to "play nice" and "don't push your brother" and "watch out for your little sister." I heard their voices, but the lady across the room had my undivided attention.

I'm pretty sure I gasped when she lifted her head. I really didn't mean to, but her face caught me completely off guard. Her jet-black hair stuck to her mascara-streaked cheeks. Her eyes were crimson red and her face was white as snow. She was crying and she was in pain and I had to go.

Our eyes met, and my heart felt the depth of her pain. Oblivious to everything around me, I grabbed a handful of napkins off my food tray and walked across the playroom to her table.

"Hi. Is it okay if I sit down? I noticed you look upset. Here are some napkins," I said in one breath, and not waiting for a yes-you-may-sit-down reply, I sat directly across from her.

And she began talking. And I tried to listen closely and follow her words, but I couldn't because it was all so confusing and "out there."

" . . . flying horses . . . fighting men . . . women screaming . . . children running . . ."

The plot to a movie, I thought. No. This was her reality. But the sadness and fear in her eyes opened a window to her soul and spoke more than her words ever could.

I didn't stop her. I didn't quote Scripture. I didn't interject my own personal story. I listened. I stepped into her reality and I held out my hand and took hers.

We sat there for quite some time, and as quickly as she'd begun to talk, she stopped. The moment was awkward. I felt her reading me like a book. She wanted something; I had no idea what. I was searching for words, but there were none.

And as she was pulling her hand away from mine, steadying herself on the table to rise and leave, the words finally found their way to my mouth: "Jesus cares. He's all I've got."

"He's a king," she said, nodding, but I'm not sure it was in agreement.

My eyes still fixed on her, I replied, "He's *the* King."

She grabbed her tray, called to her son, and walked out of the playroom. I never saw her again. I have no idea what happened to her. I'm really not sure what all happened in those moments we had together. What I do know is this: our communities are inundated with people who are full of darkness, living without hope, searching for something to fill massive voids in their hearts. They need to know there is a King. They need to know there is hope. They need us to go to them and become a part of their reality. They need us, as Jesus followers, to shine the Light into their darkness.

 e. (embrace)

How are you doing carrying light into the dark world? Can others see the light of Christ shining forth in your life? If not, what steps do you need to take to make sure you're fanning the flame of Christ's magnificent light in your life?

_____

_____

_____

_____

_____

_____

_____

_____

_____

d.i.v.e. into LESSON TWO

d. (define)

i. (investigate)

v. (visualize)

e. (embrace)

Walking in God's Wisdom

Ephesians 5:15-21

Before you begin your time of study and learning, spend a few moments in prayer asking God to give you an open heart and mind to learn new truths from His Word.

v. (visualize)

Take a snapshot of Ephesians 5 by reading through the chapter at least three times, reminding yourself of the big picture. Review your WOW from chapter 5. Don't forget to add to your outline/paraphrase.

In this lesson we're going to zoom in on Ephesians 5:15–21. As you read these verses again, begin to d.i.v.e. below the surface.

GREAT WISDOM

Read 1 Kings 3:5-14. What do you learn about Solomon from this passage?

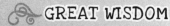

_____

_____

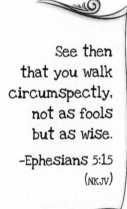

What great wisdom young Solomon unknowingly showed when he asked the Lord to give to him an understanding heart, a heart that would know how to rightly govern his people, a heart that would know right from wrong. The request greatly pleased God. In fact, it pleased Him so much that He lavishly blessed Solomon above and beyond what he'd asked for. God poured down upon him, immeasurably more than above all he asked or even thought to ask for.

> See then that you walk circumspectly, not as fools but as wise.
>
> -Ephesians 5:15 (NKJV)

Wisdom. We should all ask God to rain down showers of godly wisdom upon us, to drench us with the knowledge to walk according to the standards and precepts found in His Word.

Read Ephesians 5:15–17 from the New King James Version.

To "walk circumspectly" means to live life carefully, mindful of one's steps and the effects they will bring about. Paul encourages believers to walk not as fools, but as those who are wise, those who walk according to the standards found in the Word of God.

i. (investigate)

If wisdom is being able to discern right from wrong based on the precepts and guidelines of God's Word, what do you think walking in the way of a fool would mean?

_____

_____

_____

_____

Read the following verses. Record what they say about the foolish person.

Proverbs 1:7

_____

_____

_____

Proverbs 1:22

_____

_____

_____

Proverbs 14:9

_____

_____

_____

1 Corinthians 2:14

_____

_____

_____

Romans 1:21–22

_____

_____

_____

The fool lives a life spiritually separated from God, refusing to live his life according to the guidelines found in the Word of God. A fool doesn't understand the truths of God nor does he comprehend how lost he is, because his way is dark. Paul says believers are in no way to act as the fool, but are instead to walk as those who are full of wisdom, redeeming the time God has given them here on earth.

A REDEEMED PAST

Sometimes the truth of God's Word is hard to swallow. Sometimes it's so hard to believe God has a perfect plan for redeeming what's been lost, given up, or messed up. It's not easy to see how God's perfect plan can involve a horrific past of failures and shame. Listen, my friend: I understand. There are days when I'd like to throw in the towel and quit. Days when I feel as though I've been plowed over by a truck and left roadside to be dinner for the next hungry buzzard that flies overhead.

I have days when I can't seem to talk without crying, so I keep silent. Days when I just want to pull the covers over my head and pretend I don't exist. Days when I wonder what in the world God was thinking when He called me out from a world of darkness into His glorious light to be on mission for Him. Days when I ask why or I wallow in the what-if's of the past. Days when my self-doubt is about to swallow me whole. And days when I feel so chained to my past failures that I can't move, much less breathe.

A past of failures and hurts can do that to a person: keep you bound. Render you ineffective. Cripple you.

I'm not the only one to ever feel that way, and neither are you. Moses felt that way too. He said to God, "Who am I that I should go to Pharaoh and bring the Israelites out of Egypt?" (Exodus 3:11 NIV). Then he said, "What if they do not believe me or listen to me and say, 'The LORD did not appear to you'?" (Exodus 4:1 NIV).

Moses had a past, yet God called him. He handpicked him to be the one who would lead His chosen people from captivity to freedom. God specially selected and called Moses to redeem the time he'd been given.

God called him, but Moses responded . . .

"Me? Why? They won't listen to me. I don't know what to say. In fact, did You know I stutter? And besides that, do you know where I come from? I murdered a guy! There's no way those people are going to follow me; they know who I used to be."

Okay. So maybe he didn't *really* say those last few things, but I imagine those thoughts swirled around in his mind. Any way you look at it, Moses felt incompetent to be used by God. He felt worthless. He felt *way out of his league* to be leading "God's people" from bondage to freedom. He felt as though his time to shine was lost. Here's where I think Moses got himself into trouble (and where you and I very often do the same): *He focused on his past instead of on a future led by God.*

When Moses met God that day at the burning bush, he was comfortable with his life. But comfort wasn't what God was looking for. It was God's plan to move Moses beyond comfort into total reliance upon Him.

Moses had walked away from palace living (something good) and murder (something not so good) and settled into the here and now of his newfound life. Sure, his past surfaced every now and then, but he learned to walk right over it and not stop to harp on it.

What Moses failed to realize was that his past life experiences had readied him for the task at hand. He had yet to realize that not only did his future have purpose, but his past did as well! God planned to use the entirety of Moses' life for His good and His purpose. He would

> But now you have been united with Christ Jesus. Once you were far away from God, but now you have been brought near to him through the blood of Christ.
>
> -Ephesians 2:13 (NLT)

redeem all the hurt, all the wounds, all the shame and guilt and bitterness for His perfect will to be completed.

Every single bit of our pasts has a purpose. And it's a God-sized purpose if we allow it to be. In Christ, we've been redeemed by the blood; we have been brought back into right relationship with our heavenly Father, and now is the time for us to make the most of the time we have left here on earth. Now is the time for us to take back from the enemy the past years he stole from us and live wisely, understanding that God has a purpose and plan for our lives as new creations in Him—a plan to make our Jesus known and help set the captives free!

But how? How do we let go of our past and redeem the time we've been given?

BE FILLED WITH THE SPIRIT

Read Ephesians 5:18–21. What are believers to be filled with, and how are they to behave?

_____

_____

_____

_____

At the moment of salvation, the Holy Spirit takes up residence in the life of every believer, filling him full. Paul says we're to live under the influence of and be controlled by the Holy Spirit, yielding only to His authority. We're not to live under the influence of alcohol, which, consumed in large quantities, can leave one's mentality very much altered. Nor are we to live under the influence of drugs, sexual promiscuity, food addictions, the opinions of others, and the list could go on and on. We're to live solely under the Holy Spirit's influence.

As a result of living under the influence of the Holy Spirit, believers will reap the personal rewards of a life that joyfully sings, gives thanks, and humbly submits to other believers.

 ## e. (embrace)

I know it seems as though we keep coming back to this whole "what in your past hinders you?" question, and we do. Paul wants us to remember what we were and what we've been rescued from, and then move forward into deeper faith in Jesus. I don't know about you, but more times than not, I need the same thing beaten into my head over and over again.

So . . . what, if anything, from your past cripples you? What causes you to want to pull the covers over your head and pretend you don't exist? I firmly believe it's okay to tell God exactly how you feel, your fears, doubts, and reservations. I also believe in leaving those thoughts with Jesus, allowing Him to cover them with His blood, heal the brokenness, and redeem those times of pain. I invite you to spend time today letting go of your junk, pouring your heart out to God. Share with Him your heartaches, struggles, doubts, and reservations. And then, leave it all with Him.

_____

_____

_____

_____

_____

_____

d.i.v.e. into LESSON THREE

d. (define)

i. (investigate)

v. (visualize)

e. (embrace)

LESSON THREE

Strength in Submission
Ephesians 5:22-33

 Before you begin your time of study and learning, spend a few moments in prayer asking God to give you an open heart and mind to learn new truths from His Word.

 ### v. (visualize)

Take a snapshot of Ephesians 5 by reading through the chapter at least three times, reminding yourself of the big picture. Review your WOW from chapter 5. Don't forget to add to your outline/paraphrase.

In this lesson we're going to zoom in on Ephesians 5:22–33. As you read these verses again, begin to d.i.v.e. below the surface.

THE "S" WORD

Read Ephesians 5:22–33. Submission. It's been debated for years and years. And I can just imagine this concept will be discussed for years to come. Women submitting to men. Wives submitting to husbands. If a wife submits to her husband, does that mean she's weak? Less than? Of no value?

Absolutely not! A wife submitting to her husband reaches beyond the boundaries of being a concept and plants itself into the reality of being a command straight from God.

d. (define)

Before we move any farther, let's define the term *submit* as found in Ephesians 5:22. Using *Strong's Concordance*, define the term in the space provided.

Consider Thayer's Greek Definitions for the term *submit*:

1) to arrange under, to subordinate; 2) to subject, put in subjection; 3) to subject one's self, obey; 4) to submit to one's control; 5) to yield to one's admonition or advice; 6) to obey, be subject[1]

Biblical submission is a relinquishing of one's own desires for the sole benefit of others; it's outwardly motivated and focused on others. Worldly submission is self-serving; it's only interested in how self will come out better. It has a problem with authority and only submits when someone is watching.

CHRIST AND HIS CHURCH; A HUSBAND AND HIS WIFE

 Read Ephesians 5:23-24 from the New King James Version. True or False.

T or F—The wife is the head of the husband.

T or F—Christ is the head of the church.

T or F—Husbands and wives have joint roles as leaders of their home.

T or F—The church instructs Christ as to what He's to do.

The husband's leadership in his home is to be a reflection of Christ's leadership in the church, head over all. The church doesn't have a joint role with Christ but rather is to submit to Him. And so, too, is the wife to submit to her husband and not play a joint role as the leader of their home.

Read Ephesians 5:25-29. How is a husband to love his wife?

_____

_____

_____

_____

Husbands are to love their wives with an unselfish, undeserved, sacrificial love just as Christ loved the church. His greatest desire for his wife should be that she becomes perfectly conformed to the image of God. Just as Christ leads His church, the husband is to lead his wife to follow hard after Christ. He's to love her with a purifying love, a love that leads her away from sin and into the arms of God. He's to lavish upon her grace, making her clean through the influence of the Word of God so she can be presented as a pure and spotless bride before a holy and righteous God. A Christian husband should love his wife as much and even more than he loves his own body, a love made evident when he puts her needs above his own. The husband is to nourish his wife, helping her grow to spiritual maturity. And he is to cherish her with tender love, protecting her and comforting her.

Read Ephesians 5:30-33 and cross-reference it with Genesis 2:24. For what reason does a man leave his father and mother?

_____

_____

_____

God instituted marriage between one man and one woman at Creation. Just as the church is one with Christ, husbands and wives are to be one with each other: spiritually, emotionally, and physically. The great mystery of Jews and Gentiles becoming one in Christ was a hidden reality of the past but now has been made known to all through the New Testament church. Marriage is a divine reflection of the glorious and magnificent coming together of Christ and the church. A Christian marriage is to be a visible expression of Christ and His love for the church and the unity of that body of believers.

Now, it could be that you're thinking to yourself, _This all sounds great, but my husband is not a Christian. Do I still have to submit to him?_ May I answer this question by encouraging you to **read 1 Peter 3:1–6**? Go ahead and read it right now. Jot down your thoughts in the space provided.

_____

_____

_____

_____

_____

_____

_____

_____

Or you may be thinking, *Sounds great—but I'm not married.* Let me respond to this thought by encouraging you to **read Isaiah 54:5**. What do you learn from this verse about who your husband is?

_____

_____

_____

_____

If you're in an abusive relationship, God does NOT want you to remain in that situation. He desires that you seek a safe place and find help and healing. Love your husband from a distance, pray for him, continue to honor him as your mate, and allow God to work in his heart. God can change him and desires to do so, reuniting your family!

A CHANGED MARRIAGE

It was my fourth semester of Old Testament. I sat in the second row, fourth desk, inside a room covered from floor to ceiling with painted maps of the nation of Israel, Abraham's journeys, the Exodus, and many other pertinent Old Testament happenings. But that week the maps didn't distract me. My thoughts, eyes, and heart were completely focused on the professor as he stood behind the lectern, tears streaming down his face, and taught through the book of Hosea. I was deeply moved as we took this journey, but wouldn't completely grasp its true meaning until years later when my own husband would suffer long for my affection and love for him.

Hosea was a prophet of Yahweh. He served the Lord in ministry from 755 to 710 BC. During his years of service, the nation of Israel, God's chosen people, experienced peace, prosperity, moral corruption, and spiritual ruin. Hosea's primary focus was to open Israel's blinded spiritual eyes in hopes that they'd see how they'd violated their covenant relationship with Yahweh.

The LORD called Hosea to marry a woman who would prostitute herself during their marriage. This woman would give birth to children who may or may not be his biological offspring. She would disgrace him and bring shame upon their home. But Hosea wouldn't leave her; instead he'd stand right beside her. He'd not shun her; he'd welcome her home. He'd never hate her; instead he'd love her deeply. Hosea was the poster child of patience in a marital relationship if ever there was one.

In section 4, lesson 1, we learned that patience is a characteristic of a worthy walk. As we dove deeper into the meaning of patience, we discovered that it means "endurance, constancy, steadfastness, perseverance, forbearance, longsuffering, slowness in avenging wrongs."[2] Keep this definition in mind as we move forward.

In *John Gill's Exposition of the Entire Bible*, the author says the following about longsuffering, which is another word for patience: "Longsuffering is a patient bearing and enduring of present evils with joyfulness, being strengthened by the Spirit with all might, according to His glorious power; being slow to anger, ready to forgive injuries, put up with affronts (insults), and bear with, and forbear one another: and which is usually accompanied with gentleness, humanity, affability, courteousness, shown both in words, gestures, and actions."[3]

Hosea joyfully endured the trials in his marriage because he knew there was a greater purpose. But how was Hosea able to repeatedly forgive his wife? Why did he continue to take her back? Why didn't he just divorce her and marry a godly woman who would be faithful to him? How could his love for Gomer suffer so long?

How could he be so patient? Because patience—godly patience—has nothing to do with one's present circumstances but is solely based on the One who is in control of those circumstances.

From Galatians 5:22 we learn that patience is a result of the Holy Spirit's dwelling in and among His people—"The Holy Spirit produces . . ." Hosea was able to demonstrate patience in his marital relationship because his focus wasn't on the circumstances around him, but rather on Yahweh. Hosea wasn't keeping a running list of all the times his wife came home late. He wasn't keeping score of how many times he was right and she was wrong. Hosea remained true and faithful to the calling God placed on his life to marry

> But the fruit of the Spirit is love, joy, peace, LONGSUFFERING, kindness, goodness, faithfulness, gentleness, self-control. Against such there is no law.
>
> —Galatians 5:22-23 (NKJV; emphasis added)

Gomer. His marriage served as a reminder to all of God's covenant love for His people.

On February 13, 2003, that Old Testament classroom I'd sat in years earlier flooded my mind and left me sitting at my kitchen table, weeping over the first four years of my marriage. The words my professor shared that week about Hosea, the emotion with which he had shared of the heartache Hosea lived through, the longsuffering love this man graciously offered his wife, had now become my own reality.

You see, I had prostituted my husband's love for me; I'd corrupted it, cheapened it, and degraded him in ways I never imagined possible. I married him not because I loved him, but because I was searching for something to fill a massive void in my life, a void he couldn't fill. He didn't do things my way or treat me as I thought I deserved to be treated, so, in turn, I felt justified in not submitting to his leadership or respecting him as my husband.

I lied to him. I manipulated him. I worked late and stayed out later. He'd load up our youngest child in the middle of the night and come looking for me, worried I'd been in a car accident or something. It was never a car accident, but there was always *something* that pulled me away. I disgraced him time and time again and shamed his name when my name appeared in the arrest column of the local paper. I was his badge of dishonor.

But in his own reality of searching for something to fill his own heart voids, he was my Hosea. And he loved me. He never sought revenge. He never lost his cool. He simply endured, suffering long because he refused to give up on us . . . on me. He loved me through all my escapades, and he loved me back home. He was a picture of Jesus to me, an in-the-flesh example of sacrificial love, abundant grace, and rich mercy. He loved me as Christ loves His church: purely, selflessly, completely.

November and December of 2002 proved to be life-changing in our marriage. All the counseling in the world, all the greatest books ever written about marriage, all the opinions from others of what we should and shouldn't do to make our marriage work were pointless until we submitted ourselves to God. Until we relinquished control of our lives and submitted ourselves to the lordship of Christ, nothing in our lives would be right. I found myself one Friday night in November facedown before the Lord, confessing sins and begging for God's forgiveness. My husband found himself on our kitchen floor one Monday night in December, doing the same. And as a result of our submission to God, our hearts toward each other changed.

Submission to God enabled me to submit to my husband's leading in our marriage and family; it unified us and gave us a love for each other that we'd never had before.

The world often views a wife submitting to her husband as weak and archaic. But submitting doesn't prove weakness; it proves you have the strength to admit you know you cannot do it on your own. I think Bob Deffinbaugh said it best when he said, "Submission is the key to unity and harmony in human relationships."[4]

> submitting doesn't prove weakness; it proves you have the strength to admit you know you cannot do it on your own.

Submission is the key, not the problem. Unity, harmony, peace, and healing come into our marriages when we've submitted ourselves to God and His plan for our lives.

I asked my husband to join me in closing our lesson today. We know marriage is hard, and at times, having a good, harmonious marriage seems like an impossible feat. But we also know God can do immeasurably more than we can ask or imagine when hearts are submitted to Him. Please know we're praying for you, your spouse, and your marriage. From our hearts to yours . . .

From one wife to another:

Surrender control. Allow your husband to lead.

Acknowledge his leadership even in the small things, and thank him for all he does.

Respond to his love by loving him in return.

From one husband to another:

Love God. Let Him guide you.

Love your bride. Put her first.

Take the initiative. Be aggressive in your love.

e. (embrace)

What are your thoughts on biblical submission? Do you find yourself submitting to your husband's leadership in your home, or are you constantly nagging him to do things your way? Do you have a hard time submitting to your spouse because he's unsaved or because of hurtful things that have happened between the two of you in the past?

I encourage you to do a few things as you wrap up this lesson:

1. Seek God, asking Him to help you get to the root of why you have issues with submitting to your spouse.

2. If there's tension in your marriage, ask God to change your heart toward your spouse.

3. Write the following statement on an index card and carry it until it is burned into your heart . . .

Submission is the key to unity and
harmony in human relationships.

–Bob Deffinbaugh

4. Go hug your man and tell him you love him!

Warrior Girl

EPHESIANS SIX

d.i.v.e. into LESSON ONE

d. (define)

i. (investigate)

v. (visualize)

e. (embrace)

The Believer's Role

Ephesians 6:1-9

 Before you begin your time of study and learning, spend a few moments in prayer asking God to give you an open heart and mind to learn new truths from His Word.

 ## v. (visualize)

Take a snapshot of Ephesians 6 by reading through the chapter at least three times so you understand the big picture. As you're reading, make note of any verse(s) that tugs at your heart; this may be the WOW God is giving you from chapter 6 to embrace. Begin to develop your own outline/paraphrase.

In this lesson we're going to zoom in on Ephesians 6:1–9. As you read these verses again, begin to d.i.v.e. below the surface.

THE FAMILY UNIT

In Ephesians 5:22–33 Paul begins building for us the family unit. He clearly lays out the role of the husband and wife in relation to Christ and His bride, the church. In the first few verses of Ephesians 6, he'll continue to build for us the God-ordained design for the family.

Families are intended to be unified, kind, loving, godly, helpful, selfless, and a witness and reflection of God. List other things you believe families are intended to be.

_____

_____

God's chosen people were destined to be a people through whom "all of the families of the earth will find their blessing" (Genesis 12:3). They were commissioned to be a "kingdom of priests, a nation holy *and set apart*" (Exodus 19:6). They were to be both a recipient of God's blessings and a witness of His blessings to those around them.

i. (investigate)

Before we study through Ephesians 6:1–4, Paul's encouragement and instruction to children and parents, it's important for us to zoom out of Ephesians and look back into the book of Deuteronomy at the *Shema*.

Read Ephesians 6:1–4 and Deuteronomy 6:4–9. Grab a piece of paper and create your own d.i.v.e. form or make an extra copy of this lesson's form and d.i.v.e. into both of these passages.

THE *SHEMA*

Deuteronomy 6:4–9 is a part of the *Shema*. The *Shema* is the Jewish confession of faith made up of three parts: Deuteronomy 6:4–9; Deuteronomy 11:13–21; and Numbers 15:37–41. This confession of faith is recited twice a day by the devout Jew. The *Shema* teaches us, as parents, about our role in the spiritual rearing of our children.

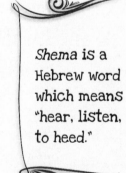

Shema is a Hebrew word which means "hear, listen, to heed."

🖋 **Reread Deuteronomy 6:4–9.** How many times are the words "you," "your," "you're," or "you'll" used?

_____

That's right; *seventeen times* in five verses, we find the word "you" or some form of it. Why is the repeated use of these pronoun forms significant? What does this mean for us as parents? It means God isn't talking to and/or commanding our pastors, our children's Sunday school teachers, or their youth leaders to be the primary ones teaching our children about Him. Now, don't get me wrong, God does call godly men and women to fill those roles, and these individuals do play a huge part in the spiritual lives of our children. But we, the parents, are the ones who are solely responsible to give our children a solid foundation and instill within them a love for Jesus. Look at what verse 5 says: "You should . . ." You should do it. I should do it. We should point our children to Jesus.

> Children can have no greater inheritance than the godly legacy left them by their parents.

Let's d.i.v.e. into Deuteronomy 6:4–9 and add to what you've already discovered. God begins by giving the parents instructions to love Him with all their hearts, minds, souls, and strength.

Read the first part of Deuteronomy 6:4.

This passage starts out with a command, a verb, an action word: *"Listen, Israel!"* God, first and foremost, instructs His people—the elders, the adults, the parents—to listen to Him *and* obey. He says, "Listen up. Open up your ears, minds, and hearts to Me. I've got some things to tell you that are of utmost importance." Let's continue reading to discover what God has to say.

Read the second part of Deuteronomy 6:4. What is it God wants us to hear? "The Eternal is our True God—He alone." This can also be translated from the original language to read, "The LORD is our God, the LORD alone (the only one)." In other words, "Hey guys, I am the only true and living God. There is no other besides Me. Those false gods, Baal and Asherah, won't do anything for you. I, alone, am God. Period. The end. That's all she wrote."

Read Deuteronomy 6:5, the second command. "You should love Him, your True God, with all your heart and soul, with every ounce of your strength." This is an intimate kind of love; the kind of love that has no boundaries and no limits. This command is ours first. As a parent, I'm to love God with every ounce of my being and strive to please Him in all that I do *before* I can lead my children to practice this in their own lives. All that is within me is to be completely filled up to overflowing with almighty God so it can spill forth from my life onto and into the lives of those closest to me.

Read Deuteronomy 6:6. Parents are to implant God's Word. "Make the things I'm commanding you today part of who you are." We're to be obeying His commands first, setting the example for our children. God's Words, His commands, precepts, statutes, and ordinances are to be engraved upon our hearts and a part of our very makeup. The only way for this to happen is for us to be actively and purposefully embracing, implanting, and enacting the Word. (See Appendix V.)

> Deep within me I have hidden Your word so that I will never sin against You.
>
> -Psalm 119:1

We're to have God's Word ever before us, whether physically, with our Bibles always open, or intellectually and relationally, with His Word in the forefront of our minds because we've implanted it deeply.

Read Deuteronomy 6:7, the third command, but this time from the New King James Version. "You shall teach them diligently to your children . . ." *Diligent* means persevering and careful in work; industrious; done with careful, steady effort; painstaking.

We should be hard at work, carefully teaching our children about the Lord. Every day, all day, everywhere we go and in everything we do, God should be our center. But how? How do we teach our children God's Word, commands, precepts, and statutes? We're given the answer right here in this verse: we're to talk about God's Word when we sit and when we walk. When we put our kids to bed at night and when they get up in the mornings, we're to be busy about living out the commands of God.

Read and then write Deuteronomy 6:7–9 in the space provided.

_____

_____

_____

_____

_____

The passages we're studying in Ephesians and Deuteronomy right now are addressed specifically to parents. But, all Scripture is "useful [for] teaching, rebuke, correction, instruction, and training" (2 Timothy 3:16) so those of you who may not have children in your home can still glean from this lesson.

Is there a teen you can pour your life into? Someone younger in the faith you can walk with and teach God's Word?

"Children" in our lives can come in a number of different ways. Let's be on the lookout for those opportunities to be godly "parents" to those God sends our way.

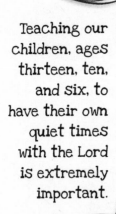 e. (embrace)

How can your family embrace and enact God's commands in Deuteronomy 6:7-9? Here are a few ways our family strives to live deeply these instructions . . .

Switching back to *The Voice* again, let's take a deeper look at these verses:

"when you're sitting together in your home . . . the next morning."

Teaching our children, ages thirteen, ten, and six, to have their own quiet times with the Lord is extremely important. Our oldest, now able to do this on her own, sits on her bed each morning and reads through her devotional book and the Scripture passage presented for that day. She writes in her journal about what she's learned and picks a verse to record on her Scripture index cards. I spend time with the younger two, reading God's Word to them and discussing its meaning. We do this first thing in the morning because I want them to know how important it is to start their days with Jesus, asking Him what His plan is for them that day. To set a positive example and because I desperately need my own personal time with Jesus, I make it a priority to rise earlier than anyone else in my home so I can spend my time with the Lord and prepare for the day.

> Teaching our children, ages thirteen, ten, and six, to have their own quiet times with the Lord is extremely important.

" . . . when you're walking together down the road."

My kids and I often take nature walks. As we walk, we talk about God's creation—about how only God Almighty, the Creator of the universe, could have created something out of nothing and made it into this beautiful place we called planet Earth. Each of the kids usually finds something (a flower, a butterfly wing, a leaf, a stick) to bring home and put in his or her nature journal. Inside their journals, right beside their newfound treasures, we'll write a verse reminding us to praise God for everything He's created for us to enjoy.

"before you go to bed . . ."

Each night, when we put our kids to bed, we pray with them. Before we pray, we ask them a few questions: "How did God bless you today? What did God show you that you need to work on today? Is there anything you need to confess to the Lord and repent of before you go to sleep?"

"Do whatever it takes to remember them: **tie a reminder on your hand and bind a reminder on your forehead** *where you'll see it all the time."*

My kids and I often take nature walks. As we walk, we talk about God's creation-about how only God Almighty, the Creator of the universe, could have created something out of nothing and made it into this beautiful place we called planet Earth.

Throughout Jewish history, people took this act literally by tying phylacteries (little boxes containing these verses) around their arms or strapping them to their foreheads. Often, phylacteries were worn on the upper arms so that when one crossed his arms in prayer, God's Word would be closest to his heart. Phylacteries aren't seen much today, but we make it common practice in our home to memorize Scripture. Our kids have both Scripture journals and spiral-bound index cards upon which they write out verses they're hiding in their hearts.

"[Write them on] the doorpost where you cross the threshold or on the city gate."

Scripture is everywhere in our home. Some verses are beautifully framed, some are cute little things I've printed from the computer, and others are index cards taped to bathroom mirrors. Whether it be a Scripture card on the back of the front door that we can read as we leave reminding us to "let our light shine before men," a card on the inside of the entertainment center urging us to "turn away our eyes from worthless things," or a card on the bathroom mirror telling us the "King is enthralled with our beauty," God's Word has a place everywhere in our home and in every aspect of our lives.

The *Shema*. The Jewish confession of faith. A declaration of faith in one God. A pronouncement to love God with all your heart, soul, and strength. A command to hear, heed, and obey the truths contained within the Word of God.

The *Shema* . . .

For the parent . . . LISTEN to God,
LOVE God, FOLLOW God, TEACH
God's Word to your children.

For the child . . . learn to LISTEN to God,
learn to LOVE God, learn to FOLLOW
God, learn to TEACH God's Word.

My children will one day stand before the Lord, as will I, and answer directly to Him regarding how they've lived their lives, under His leading or according to their own selfish desires. It's my responsibility and privilege as their parent to bring them up in a home that has God as its foundation. I'm to teach them the ways of God, love them with the love of the Lord, and discipline them according to God's Word. Ultimately, I cannot make them follow the Lord, but it's my responsibility to do all I can to aid them in traveling down the straight and narrow.

Let's zoom back in on our passage in Ephesians.

d.i.v.e. DEEPER . . . BRINGING THEM UP IN THE DISCIPLINE OF GOD

Reread Ephesians 6:4. Review and add to your d.i.v.e. from earlier on in this lesson.

_____

_____

_____

_____

_____

_____

Note: In Ephesians 6:1-3, Paul addresses both parents, using the Greek word *goneus* meaning "a *parent:* parent (vs. 1, parent); patēr meaning a "father" (literally or figuratively, near or more remote): father, parent (vs. 2, father); and mētēr a "mother" (literally or figuratively, immediate or remote): mother (vs. 2, mother)."[1]

In Ephesians 6:4, his message seems to be aimed only to fathers, but if we dive below the surface into the original meaning of *father* here, we'll discover that Paul uses, again, the Greek word *patēr*, meaning "a 'father' (literally or figuratively, near or more remote): father, parent."[2]

> My children will one day stand before the Lord, as will I, and answer directly to Him regarding how they've lived their lives, under His leading or according to their own selfish desires.

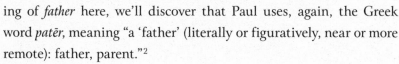

I'm bringing this to our attention because it's clear that Paul is speaking not only to the father, but the mother as well. Let's keep this in mind as we move forward into the next verses.

Here we're introduced to *patria potestas*, Latin for "power of a father." Under Roman family law, a father had, literally, life-and-death power over his children. When a child was born, he or she was placed at the father's feet. If the father picked up the child, that child was allowed to stay in the home. If the father walked away from the newborn, he or she was discarded. Healthy children who'd been discarded were taken each night to the town forum, where they'd be chosen and raised by slaves or prostitutes.

Paul, being a Roman citizen, understood *patria potestas*. I'm sure he'd seen it practiced over and over again growing up. He knew firsthand the great influence and power a father had over his children's physical lives. When Paul wrote to the Ephesian believers, encouraging them not to provoke their children to anger (ESV), but to bring them up in the discipline and teaching of the Lord, he had the children's physical, emotional, and spiritual lives in mind.

 ## d. (define)

Using a concordance or dictionary, define *provoke* as found in the New King James Version. Based on this definition, what does it mean to provoke a child to anger?

_____

_____

_____

_____

_____

What are some ways children can be provoked to anger?

_____

_____

_____

_____

Children can be pushed to anger for a number of reasons: overbearing parents, favoritism shown among siblings, being pushed to overachieve, never hearing a compliment or word of encouragement, and so forth. Paul tells us we aren't to provoke our children to anger but are to bring them up in the discipline and teaching of the Lord. God's discipline and teaching are structured and purposed; therefore, the discipline we give to our children should be administered in the same way.

The key to right and profitable discipline is administering it as the Lord would and according to His Word. We're to discipline and instruct our children with the guidance and in the power of the Holy Spirit. All discipline should be done to bring about heart change that will ultimately lead to behavior change.

IN THE WORKPLACE

Read Ephesians 6:5–8. To whom is Paul speaking?

_____

To whom are slaves to be obedient? How are they to be obedient?

_____

_____

_____

_____

Are slaves to work to please men or God? Search the Scriptures to find other verses that support your answer.

_____

_____

_____

_____

Read Ephesians 6:9. How are masters to treat their slaves? Why are they to show no partiality?

_____

_____

_____

_____

A master/slave relationship seems harsh in our minds, but in Paul's day this type of language was easily understood because it was a cultural practice. In our day this concept can easily be applied to the workplace. Christian employees should be more productive and more responsible in their work than anyone else, because ultimately, they're working for God, not man. They should set a godly example for both their coworkers and those to whom they answer. Christian employers should make the work environment welcoming to all, promoting unity and honest work. They should lead by example, show no favoritism among their employees, and be respectful of those they manage.

 e. (embrace)

Paul ends his instruction on "submitting to one another in the fear of God" (NKJV) that was begun in Ephesians 5:21 with this truth: There is no partiality or favoritism in the body of Christ, because we all have a common Master, God. The husband and wife, parent and child, and employee and employer are all to be mutually submissive because they are equally loved.

As a believer, how can you begin to change the often misunderstood idea of submission and equality, reflecting its biblical foundation in your marriage, home, workplace, and church?

_____

_____

_____

_____

_____

d.i.v.e. into LESSON TWO

d. (define)

i. (investigate)

v. (visualize)

e. (embrace)

Where's the Love?

Ephesians 6:10-17

 Before you begin your time of study and learning, spend a few moments in prayer asking God to give you an open heart and mind to learn new truths from His Word.

 v. (visualize)

Take a snapshot of Ephesians 6 by reading through the chapter at least three times, reminding yourself of the big picture. Is there a WOW you're embracing and implanting in your heart? Take a few moments to review that verse(s). Don't forget to add to your outline/paraphrase.

In this lesson we're going to zoom in on Ephesians 6:10–17. As you read these verses again, begin to d.i.v.e. below the surface.

AND NOW . . . THE BATTLE BEGINS

John MacArthur says, "The true Christian described in Ephesians 1–3 who lives the faithful life described in 4:1–6:9 can be sure that he will be involved in the spiritual warfare described in 6:10–20."[1]

Satan hates God's children

Read **Ephesians 6:10–13**. Paul instructs believers to put on the armor of God. Why? Against whom are we fighting?

_____

_____

_____

_____

God's children are in the midst of a battle. And it's a battle unlike any other—a battle that puts us face-to-face with an enemy who deeply hates us and desires to destroy us from the inside out. Why does Satan hate us so? Why does he desire to render us ineffective for the kingdom of God?

Satan hates God's children because we've been rescued from his grasp by God. Through the death of Christ on the cross, believers have been set free from a life controlled by the enemy. God has chosen us to do His work and walk worthy of the calling to which we have been called through the power of the Holy Spirit working in and through us.

Read **1 Peter 2:9 and write it here.**

_____

_____

_____

_____

In Old Testament days people were unable to approach God directly. A priest acted as an intermediary between God and man. But because of Christ's victory on the cross, we can now come directly into God's presence.

Read John 8:12 and write it here.

_____

_____

_____

_____

We've been called out of a life of darkness, sin, and destruction into a life fueled by the glorious light of life, the Light of the world. We're to walk in this Light so others see and come to know the Light personally.

But Satan has a plan to destroy every Christian.

Read 2 Corinthians 11:3:

> But now I'm afraid that as that serpent tricked Eve with his wiles, so your _hearts and_ minds will be tricked and you will stray from the single-minded love and pure devotion to Him.

Paul worried that the Corinthian believers would be led astray from their single-minded devotion to God.

His worry for his friends reminds me of an old plow horse. Before the days of mechanical plows, when a farmer worked his horse, he placed a harness over its head, buckling it beneath the horse's jaw. On each side of the harness was a sight blinder that rested beside the horse's eye. The purpose of the blinders was to keep the animal focused on the task before him, instead of being distracted by everything else that was going on.

Satan desperately tries to divert the believer's attention off of God and onto something else. We must put on our spiritual blinders so we aren't easily distracted by his scheming and games.

e. (embrace)

 What are the things, people, and activities that cause your eyes to turn away from God?

_____

_____

_____

_____

Satan also hates God's children because we can lead others to Jesus.

 Read Matthew 28:19–20. What command did Jesus leave His followers?

_____

Christ commanded the disciples to go into all the world and make disciples. This command didn't stop with the first disciples; it applies to you and me today. We're to go into the entire world, into our homes, our workplaces, our children's schools, local restaurants, gas stations, parks—everywhere—sharing with everyone the message of the Gospel. It boils Satan's blood when we share Jesus, because his desire is to keep as many as he can blinded to God's saving grace.

 e. (embrace)

What are some ways you can share your Jesus story with others? What Scripture verses would you lead a person to who doesn't know Jesus personally? Maybe sharing your story with others seems a little scary to you. May I suggest you write down your story? Work it out on paper so that it's easier to speak to others. Here's a simple way to break down your story . . .

My life before Jesus . . .

_____

_____

_____

_____

_____

How I came to know Jesus . . .

_____

_____

_____

_____

_____

How my life has changed since I said yes to following Jesus . . .

_____

_____

_____

_____

_____

Never be afraid to share with others your story of how Jesus rescued you, but know that when you do, Satan will be furious and will come against you hard (2 Corinthians 5:20; Ephesians 6:20).

Bottom line . . . Satan hates God's children and does everything he can to render us ineffective for kingdom work. He's doing all he can to divert our attention off of God.

CAN WE STAND STRONG?

What can we do about Satan's attacks? Can we stand strong? In Matthew 4:1–11, Matthew gives us an example of one who stood strong against the enemy's attack. **Read this passage and d.i.v.e. deeper into it, jotting down your thoughts here.**

_____

_____

_____

_____

God made it possible for us to be protected against the enemy's attacks; Jesus is our proof. He's given us extremely powerful armor, and when it is properly worn and used, victory is sure to come.

Paul recognized the battle that raged and wanted to be sure all believers knew of the protective gear available to them. But we must go beyond just knowing about this gear. We must put it on. There's no reason for us to live discouraged, defeated lives. We have the equipment needed to fight victoriously. So let's gear up for battle!

SUITING UP

Read Ephesians 6:10–13. Why should we put on the full armor?

_____

_____

_____

_____

We aren't fighting against flesh and blood but against impish tyrants, devilish authorities, supernatural powers, and demon princes. Our enemy is spiritual; thus the battle we're in is spiritual. Therefore, we need spiritual power and spiritual protection to fight in this war.

Paul tells us we're to put on the FULL armor of God, because it's the full armor that enables us to stand our ground and fight victoriously against the enemy.

VICTORY COMES IN THE PREPARATION

Paul lived during the time of the Roman Empire, a great power structure in its day. Its armies were fierce and its soldiers indestructible fighters. Because the Ephesian church would relate to this idea of armies and battles and great fighters, Paul used this concept as a model to teach them about God's protective gear. For you see, success in battle was impossible if a soldier stepped out onto the battlefield in his everyday clothes; the victory came in his preparation.

We, too, must prepare for battle; we must put on the whole armor of God so we're able to fight.

 Read Ephesians 6:14–15. What three pieces of armor does this passage tell us to put on?

_____

_____

_____

_____

the band of truth

Read the first part of Ephesians 6:14:

The first piece of armor needed for battle was the band or belt. A soldier wore a long tunic with holes cut out for his head and arms. Because he was engaged in hand-to-hand combat, his tunic (a long shirt) needed to be "girded," as the New King James puts it; hence, a

soldier's need for a belt. This belt was a thick, leather strap used not only to gird up the tunic but also to hold weapons and tools. The soldier's belt held everything in its right place.

What do you think the Christian's "truth band" or "belt of truth" is?

_____

_____

The truth belt is the truth of God's Word; it's the knowledge that when we become Christians, everything about the way we think and live is filtered through a new set of standards—God's standards. Not only do we think and live our lives differently, but our attitudes are different as well. We know who we are in Christ, and knowing this truth enables us to enter into battle with nothing weighing on our minds; it allows us to focus because everything is tucked away and taken care of.

This new way of thinking is based on the life and teaching of Jesus, who *is* Truth. Satan wants us to believe nothing but lies, but lies only keep us in bondage. By putting on the truth band, we're empowered to reject the enemy's lies and walk in Christ's freedom.

Read John 8:32. What do you think Jesus meant when He said, "You will know the truth"? What is this "truth" He speaks of?

_____

_____

_____

_____

_____

_____

What did Jesus mean when He said, "That truth will give you freedom"?

_____

_____

_____

Read John 8:36:

So *think of it this way:* if the Son comes to make you free, you will really be free.

In this verse the first "free" is the Greek word *eleutheroo*, which means "'to liberate,' that is (figuratively), to *exempt* (from moral, ceremonial or mortal liability): deliver, make free." But the second "free" is the Greek word *eleutheros* which means "'unrestrained' (to *go* at pleasure), that is, (as a citizen) *not a slave* (whether *freeborn* or *manumitted*), or (generally) *exempt* (from obligation or liability): free (man, woman), at liberty."[2]

My friend, as a follower of Jesus, you are liberated from the enemy's lies, free from his grip. And you are no longer his slave. You are *free*! That is truth!

Knowing the truth of who Christ is and resting in the truth of what He's done for us enables us to live in the abundant freedom His death afforded us.

List some examples of truths that make up the truth belt. I'll get you started.

- We were made for God.

- Our purpose and worth are found in Christ.

- We are called to live lives of surrender and complete obedience to the leading of the Holy Spirit.

- _____
- _____

The Roman soldier only loosened his belt when he was off duty. As Christians, should we ever loosen our belts of truth? Are we ever off duty?

_____

_____

Satan's desire is to trip us up, to entangle us, to make us fall. If we aren't girded up with the truth belt, we'll do just that, fall flat on our faces in defeat.

the chest plate of righteousness

The second piece of armor the soldier needed to wear was the chest plate. The chest plate was made of strong metal, leather, or heavy linen, onto which were sewn pieces of animal hooves, horns, or metal. Each chest plate was shaped to fit the soldier's upper body, covering him from the neck to the waist, front and back; its purpose was to protect the heart and other vital organs.

Read the second part of Ephesians 6:14. What do you think the Christian's "chest plate of righteousness" is?

_____

_____

The believer's chest plate of righteousness is his righteousness in Christ (2 Corinthians 5:21) and the righteous life that he lives (Ephesians 4:24). The chest plate of Christ is given to the believer; from the *very moment* of his salvation, he's covered by the beautiful righteousness of Christ.

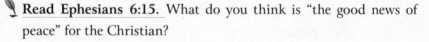 How do you think the chest plate of righteousness protects the Christian?

_____

_____

The chest plate protects our hearts; it protects our identity in Christ. Satan would like to "guilt us" and shame us over past sin, but when we have on the chest plate of Christ's righteousness, we can be confident that we're holy and acceptable to God.

the shoes of the good news of peace

The Roman soldier needed special footwear for battle. He wore sandals that were strapped tightly around his feet and ankles, giving him secure footing, a solid foundation. These shoes provided support for running and fighting. The soles would be covered with metal or nails, like cleats, giving him better traction for running and climbing.

Read Ephesians 6:15. What do you think is "the good news of peace" for the Christian?

_____

_____

The good news of peace is two-fold. First, the good news of peace is the Gospel, that is, Christ's death on the cross in our place. Because of Christ's death, believers now have peace with God. Our foundation of peace with God gives us the go-ahead to share the good news of peace with those with whom we come in contact so they, too, can experience that same peace. Second, the good news of peace is the realization that we're completely accepted by God, a realization that gives us an overwhelming sense of peace that passes all understanding even in the midst of Satan's attacks.

Read Philippians 4:6–7. What must we do to experience peace even in the midst of Satan's attacks?

_____

_____

_____

Now read the end of verse 5 and fill in the blank.

The Lord is _____.

The Lord is ever present. And because the Lord is present, we can turn our worries into prayers. We don't have to be anxious in the midst of the battle. Because the Lord is present, we can voice our concerns to Him and He will hear. The peace of God "will stand watch over your hearts and minds in Jesus" (Philippians 4:7).

True peace is not found in positive thinking, in the absence of conflict, or in good feelings; it comes from knowing and trusting that God is in control. No matter how hard things may get, we can take comfort in knowing that we can have the peace of God in our hearts and minds.

Read Ephesians 6:16–17. What are the final three pieces of armor that we must "take up" (NIV) or put on?

_____

_____

_____

The first three pieces of armor, the belt, chest plate, and shoes, were never taken off on the battlefield. The last three pieces, the shield, helmet, and sword, were kept in readiness for when the actual fighting began, hence the verb phrase "take up."

the shield of faith

A soldier's shield covered his entire body. The shield was about four and a half feet high and two and a half feet wide, made of wood, and covered with metal or heavy oiled leather. Its main purpose was to protect the body from the enemy's darts (NKJV). Because these arrows had been dipped in pitch and set on fire, a soldier would crouch behind his shield so he wouldn't be hit by the flaming darts.

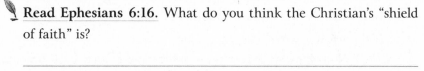 **Read Ephesians 6:16.** What do you think the Christian's "shield of faith" is?

_____

_____

_____

Satan hurls fiery darts at us all the time, and we must protect ourselves. The shield is available to us when we choose, by faith, to accept and believe that God is truly our Protector. The Roman soldier's shield was large enough to protect him entirely from the fiery darts of the enemy. God, the Christian's Shield of Faith, is larger-than-life and offers to us complete protection from our enemy, Satan.

The "faith" of this shield is a living and active faith, a faith that lives out its trust in God by clinging to the truths of God's Word, His promises, and His power. To use it, we must _believe_ that God is who He says He is and will do what He says He will do. This shield is useless if we don't actively have faith in God. We have to take it up, telling Satan we're trusting God to protect us and see us through the battle. And sometimes we might just need to spit in his face . . .

 ★ ★ ★

There's a hill. Just around the corner from my house.

We drive up and down that hill all the time. And I've walked it a handful of times. Believe me when I say the incline will work your backside and make your legs burn something fierce. Mind you, it's nothing like climbing Mt. Everest or Mt. Kilimanjaro in the least, but for me, it's a challenge.

I've wanted to run this hill for quite some time. I've stood at its bottom looking upwards, longing to make it to the top victoriously. But, I've been too afraid. And, he told me I couldn't do it. So, I settled for just . . . walking.

Ya know, he's pretty good at telling me I can't. He's done it all my life. The enemy. Satan. He's a jerk! He has this nasty habit of throwing fiery darts at me and whispering things in my ear . . .

You're too stupid.

You're fat! Nobody's gonna ask you to the prom!

He married you, but he doesn't really love you.

You're a horrible mother!

You'll never have any "real" friends.

Go ahead and take those pills . . . no one will even notice you're gone.

All these skeletons in your closet? They make you who you are.

You're worthless. Ugly. A loser.

God? He doesn't love you. Never has, never will.

So, when he told me I couldn't run up that hill I believed him . . . until recently!

Cause ya see, God's been speaking into the deep places of my heart. Pulling me deeper into the protection of His shield. Loving on me. Esteeming me. Showering me with much grace.

"I am Yours and You are mine," He said to me. And at that moment I knew the enemy was no longer going to hit me with those fiery darts of self-doubt, timidity, and fear.

It was a Wednesday morning in January. I called out to my three kids to get their tennis shoes on because we were going for a jog.

We stood at the bottom of the hill. I was confident. I was going to do this.

Then the enemy began throwing his fiery darts, whispering in my ear, *"You will never make it to the top. You can't do it!"*

I ignored him, standing strong, protected by the shield of faith that surrounded me.

"All right guys, we're gonna run to the top," I told my kids.

"You'll stop halfway there. You can't do it."

"It's going to be hard, but we can do this because God's gonna give us the strength."

"God isn't gonna do anything for you. You'll never make it."

He was really starting to make me mad.

"Everybody ready?" My kids screamed, "READY!" And we were off. Me jogging. Them running, skipping, laughing, having a great time.

We jumped over the speed bump, and then the incline began.

I could still hear that creep. He was laughing, *"You're gonna stop. You're not gonna make it."*

I was beyond mad. Furious. The arrows were flying and I was fighting hard.

I pushed harder. And his voice got louder: *"You will never . . . "*

"I CAN DO ALL THINGS IN CHRIST, YOU CREEP. LEAVE ME ALONE!" And I spit (literally) in his face because I was sick of his crap.

His voice began to fade and I pushed even harder, clinging tightly to my shield of faith, believing God was going to get me to the top of my mini mountain. It hurt. I couldn't breathe very well. My legs were on fire. I saw the stop sign. It was in reach. We were almost to the top. I KNEW I could make it. I KNEW WE could make it, God, me, and my kids.

And, we did. We made it to the top, VICTORIOUSLY! And you know what? We did it again. Yep! We all ran up that hill again. And I never heard the whispers of the enemy saying I couldn't do it.

Hills. Mountains. They're a past, present, and future thing. We're all going to stand at the bottom of a hill at some point in our lives and be faced with the climb. Let's not stand there doubting, allowing the fiery darts of the enemy to hit us, convincing us we can't make it to the top. Because, here's the truth . . .

We are God's and He is ours and His shield is big enough to cover us all and we're going to actively believe that we CAN do ALL things through His strength. ALL things!

It may be painful. It may burn something fierce. But we CAN make it through, up, and over. We can. And if we need to spit in that creep's face on the way up and scream and yell, there's no shame in that. Go right ahead and do it; it's very freeing!

I can do all things through Christ who strengthens me.

–Philippians 4:13 (NKJV)

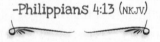

 e. (embrace)

Think on this . . . If the size of your shield is based on how much you have faith in (believe, trust) God, then how big (or small) is your shield? Do you believe God enough to be protected from the enemy's fiery darts?

What kinds of fiery darts does Satan shoot at you?

_____

_____

_____

Don't shrink back in fear; stand strong; rest in the shelter of the Most High, and abide in the shadow of the Almighty.

d.i.v.e. DEEPER . . . GOD'S PROTECTION

The Bible speaks over and over again of God's protection. **Read the following Scriptures. In the space provided, jot down what you learn about God's protection over His people from each passage.**

Psalm 91

_____

_____

Romans 8:31

_____

_____

Romans 8:38–39

_____

_____

1 Corinthians 10:13

_____

_____

Hebrews 10:17

_____

_____

the helmet of salvation

One of the most exposed parts of the human body is the head, the command center. The helmet, meant to protect the soldier's head, was made of thick leather covered with metal plates, and usually had cheek pieces to protect the face. When worn properly, the helmet protected the soldier from the double-edged sword of the enemy, which could very easily decapitate him.

Read the first six words of Ephesians 6:17. What do you think the Christian's "helmet of salvation" is?

_____

_____

The helmet of salvation is designed to protect our minds from discouragement and the doubt that our salvation isn't powerful enough to rescue us from the power of Satan's dominion. Think about it this way: Satan swings his double-edged sword our way desiring to cut us off from God. As he did with Eve, he tries to get us to doubt God, and to discourage us. Satan wants us to believe our salvation isn't strong enough to save us from his power. However, Paul addresses this lie in Colossians 1:13:

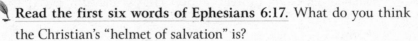

You have rescued us from dark powers and brought us safely into the kingdom of Your Son, whom You love.

🖋 Under what power were we before Christ rescued us?

_____

🖋 Because we've received salvation, where are we now?

_____

The Bible is very clear that our salvation is strong enough to save us from Satan's power and strong enough to cause him to flee.

🖋 **Read James 4:7 and write it here.**

_____

_____

_____

🖋 If we stand against Satan, what will he do?

_____

🖋 What are some ways that Satan discourages you?

_____

_____

_____

Satan wants to confuse us. He wants us to doubt God. And if he is successful, we become discouraged, defeated, and ineffective. With the helmet of salvation placed securely on our heads, we'll be protected from Satan's schemes.

the Sword of the Spirit

The band or belt, chest plate, shoes, shield, and helmet protect the soldier, but his ultimate goal is victory. And for there to be victory, the soldier must be ready to attack his enemy.

The sword was between six and eighteen inches in length. It was carried in a sheath or scabbard that was attached to the soldier's

belt. Usually, it was a two-edged sword, meaning both sides were sharpened so that it cut both ways. The sword was a symbol of power and fear to all of the empire's enemies. Ephesians 6 tells us God has armed Christians with a powerful sword that is to be feared by our enemy.

Read the second part of Ephesians 6:17. The Christian's "sword of the Spirit" is the Word of God. Why do you think Paul calls the Word of God a "sword"?

_____

_____

Read Hebrews 4:12 and write it here.

_____

_____

_____

The sword of the Spirit, the living and active Word of God, cuts the enemy's lies in half.

Christ set the example for us as to how important it is to know the Word. When Satan tempted Jesus in the wilderness (Matthew 4), it was the Word of God Jesus spoke in order to cut though Satan's lies.

You and I must be equipped with the truth of God's Word. If we want to be winners in the battle, we must know how to use the sword and d.i.v.e. deep into its truths, implanting it in our hearts.

Thomas Guthrie, a Scottish pastor and writer, said:

The Bible is an armory of heavenly weapons, a laboratory of infallible medicine, a mine of exhaustless wealth. It is a guidebook for every road, a chart for every sea, a medicine for every malady, and a balm for every wound. Rob us of our Bible and our sky has lost its sun.[3]

The sword is the only weapon God has provided to cut down all of Satan's lies. Only by making God's Word a regular part of our lives will we become the warriors we need to be.

 ## e. (embrace)

What lies of the enemy are you battling today? Are you feeling defeated because of sin? Does Satan whisper in your ear that you'll never have victory over your anger, depression, or struggling marriage? Does he tell you your wayward children will never come back to God? Maybe he dangles past addictions in your face and tells you you'll never be free from them. Or maybe he says to you that the deep pains from the past can never be healed. Oh, sweet friend, the sword of the Spirit, the truth of God's Word, can cut to smithereens the lies of the enemy.

Spend the rest of today cutting the enemy with your sword. Speak these truths aloud, and watch him flee!

- 1 Corinthians 10:13: "Any temptation you face will be nothing new. But God is faithful, and He will not let you be tempted beyond what you can handle. But He always provides a way of escape so that you will be able to endure *and keep moving forward.*"

- Philippians 3:13–14: "I know I have not arrived; but there's one thing I am doing: I'm leaving my old life behind, putting everything on the line for this mission. I am sprinting toward the only goal that counts: *to cross the line,* to win the prize, and to hear God's call *to resurrection life found exclusively* in Jesus the Anointed."

- Romans 8:1–2: "Therefore, now no condemnation awaits those who are living in Jesus the Anointed, ... because when you live in the Anointed One, Jesus, *a new law takes effect.* The law of the

Spirit of life *breathes into you and* liberates you from the law of sin and death."

- 2 Corinthians 10:5: "We are demolishing arguments and ideas, every high-and-mighty philosophy that pits itself against the knowledge of *the one true* God. We are taking prisoners of every thought, *every emotion*, and subduing them into obedience to the Anointed One."

- John 8:32: "You will know the truth, and that truth will give you freedom."

- Galatians 5:16: "Walk in the Spirit, and let the Spirit bring order to your life. If you do, you will never give in to your selfish and sinful cravings."

- 1 Peter 5:8: "Be disciplined and stay on guard. Your enemy the devil is prowling around outside like a roaring lion, just waiting *and hoping for the chance* to devour someone."

Satan is defeated, but he still hates Christians and is trying desperately to deceive us. He's constantly tempting us to rebel against God through our own sin nature and to embrace his evil system of values in this world. But God, who is rich in mercy because of His great love for us, has given us protective spiritual armor. When we use it, all of Satan's schemes and devices are useless.

 e. (embrace)

God wants us to understand we're His warrior girls, fighting in the battle of our lives. He also wants us to know He's given us the protection we need to stand strong against the enemy. But we must prepare. Are you girded up with the truth banded around your waist, armed with the chest plate of righteousness, feet protected in preparation to proclaim the good news of peace? Are you holding up your shield of faith, securing on your head the helmet of salvation, tightly holding the sword of the Spirit? Spend some time today devising your battle plan.

_____

_____

_____

_____

_____

d.i.v.e. into LESSON THREE

d. (define)

i. (investigate)

v. (visualize)

e. (embrace)

Pray Without Ceasing

Ephesians 6:18-24

 Before you begin your time of study and learning, spend a few moments in prayer asking God to give you an open heart and mind to learn new truths from His Word.

 ### v. (visualize)

Take a snapshot of Ephesians 6 by reading through the chapter at least three times, reminding yourself of the big picture. Review your WOW from chapter 6. Don't forget to add to your outline/paraphrase.

In this lesson we're going to zoom in on Ephesians 6:18–24. As you read these verses again, begin to d.i.v.e. below the surface.

DEAR JESUS,

Read Ephesians 6:18. Prayer is the closing theme of Ephesians and is much more than a piece of armor that's to be worn by a soldier in battle. While we wear the belt, the chest plate, the shoes, the shield, the helmet, and the sword, we're to be in prayer. The pieces of armor can be taken on and off, so to speak, but prayer is to be continual.

I'm not going to lie; prayer has always been hard for me, and the thought of being in prayer continually seems like drudgery to me. It just seems so . . . formal, almost like writing a business letter to the CEO of a major corporation.

> Dear Father in heaven,
> Thou art holy. I praise Thee for all Thy blessings
> Thou hast bestowed upon me. Blah, blah, blah . . .
> In the name of Jesus, and most sincerely Thine,
> Thy humble servant,
>
> me

I mean, come on; how impersonal and forced is that? And it's not only the formality of the language that gets me, but you have to bow your head, close your eyes, and talk—out loud—to Someone who isn't physically there. Really? Too much for me!

So I chose not to pray. I chose to keep my words to myself, my head up, and my eyes open. Yeah, I voiced some words before I taught my seventh grade Sunday school class. I led the group of tween girls I mentored in an opening prayer before we did our book study. And I prayed for the ladies in my accountability group when it was my turn in the circle. But the words were rehearsed and flowery and meaningless. Prayer was a religious event of useless words and wasted time—until God whacked me over the head and spoke directly into my heart.

★ ★ ★

It was Disciple Now Weekend for our junior high students. We headed to the beach that Friday afternoon with close to a hundred sixth, seventh, and eighth graders. Excitement and laughter filled the bus as we made the two-hour journey. With luggage unloaded, dinner eaten, and small groups announced, we made our way to the conference room that would be our worship area for the weekend.

As the message was coming to a close, I made my way to the back of the room to pray, because that's what leaders are supposed to do . . . pray for those they lead. I knelt. I bowed my head. I closed my eyes. And I began the formality of praying to Someone I couldn't see.

"Dear heavenly Father,

"I lift up these students to You right now. Speak to their hearts. Work in their lives. Keep us safe, and You know that thing people keep telling me I should do, the thing I love and really would like to do? Well, how about You, if You're really listening to me, tell me to do it."

It was in those next few minutes, kneeling alone in the back of a crowded room, that God spoke so clearly there was no doubt in my mind nor in my heart He was there, right beside me, listening, working, and making Himself vividly real.

The instruction from God to me was as plain as day. "Maybe God is telling you to write your story," the student pastor said. And I knew those words were for me because, I found out later, no one else heard them and God had already been speaking that message into my heart for months, but I was sure He'd been talking to the wrong person. Sure He meant this message for someone else. Sure He wouldn't talk directly to me. But God answered my pleading heart because He knew I needed that extra bit of assurance. He knew I need Him to be tangibly real in my life. He knew I needed that word spoken straight into my heart.

God and I connected in the deep places of my heart that Friday night. The reality that He actually heard my words and actively responded was another proof positive that He was ever working in me. Prayer became my lifeline to the beating of His heart. Nothing about

Prayer is the very spiritual air that the soldier of Christ breathes. It is the all-pervasive strategy in which warfare is fought.

–John MacArthur [1]

my praying was ever formal again, nor is it an event of meaningless chatter. Prayer is my connection to the heart of God, a connection I never interrupt, talking to Him whenever I can, and wherever I am.

Read 1 Thessalonians 5:17. What does this verse tell you about praying?

_____

When the battle gets hard, it's very easy for us to become disheartened. Jesus encourages us to always stay in communication with Him and not lose heart, especially during these times (Luke 18:1). In the throes of battle, prayer is our lifeline.

REMEMBERING GOD'S BLESSINGS

Throughout Ephesians Paul has beautifully laid out for us all the believer has been blessed with. **Looking back at Ephesians 1:3–6:17, list all the believer's blessings, along with their references.**

_____

_____

_____

_____

It would be very easy for us to look at our list of blessings and feel confident that we'll be able to stand in our own strength against the enemy. There is great danger here for spiritual arrogance.

Read 1 Corinthians 10:12 and write it here.

_____

_____

_____

Satan will do his best to get us to focus on the blessings we've been given instead of the One who has blessed us with those gifts. We can very easily begin to think we're good to go with these gifts and in the process of moving ahead leave the Gift Giver behind. This is exactly why Paul says we're to stay in constant communication with God.

Ephesians lifts believers to the heavenly places and then brings them to their knees before the Father. The spiritual armor won't work, won't make us victorious in battle, without God being the One to supply it.

Read Ephesians 6:18 again, this time from the New King James Version. How are we to pray?

_____

_____

_____

d. (define)

What is the difference between a prayer and supplication?

_____

_____

_____

When Paul says, "With all prayer and supplication," he's speaking to general prayers (prayer) and specific prayers, or pleas (supplication).

d.i.v.e. DEEPER . . . HOW AND WHEN?

Pray at all times. **Read Psalm 55:17, 19; Luke 21:36; and Acts 2:42.** What do these verses teach about prayer?

_____

_____

_____

_____

_____

Pray in the Spirit. **Read Romans 8:26–27.** What do these verses teach about prayer?

_____

_____

> The Spirit is the fuel that ignites our prayers to burn in accordance to the will of God.

_____

_____

    Only in the Spirit's power can we pray according to the will of God; otherwise our prayers would be self-centered and focused only on what we want and think we deserve. The Spirit is the fuel that ignites our prayers to burn in accordance with God's will.

Pray with a watchful eye. **Read Mark 14:38.** What does it teach about prayer?

_____

_____

Pray persistently. **Read Acts 1:14; 2:42; 6:4; and Romans 12:12.** What do these verses teach about prayer?

_____

_____

_____

_____

_____

Pray for all the body of Christ. **Read 1 Samuel 12:23; Philippians 1:3–4; Colossians 1:9; and James 5:16.** What do these verses teach about prayer?

_____

_____

_____

_____

_____

_____

PRAYING FOR LEADERS

Read Ephesians 6:19–20. Paul told the Ephesian believers how to pray in verse 18. What does he ask them to do in verses 19 and 20?

_____

Paul simply asked them to pray for him. Remember he was in prison as he wrote this letter. He didn't ask the Ephesians to pray he be released; he only asked that they pray he'd be bold in his

proclamation of the Gospel. Yes, he was in chains physically, but he was bound by something far more powerful than those chains; he was bound up in Christ and committed to the mission. Paul wanted his friends to pray he'd be victorious in the spiritual battle he was in.

As a leader, he especially needed their prayers because when a leader is attacked and falls, those under his care often scatter (Matthew 26:13). Leaders are Satan's prime target because more people are affected when they're wounded.

Take time right now to pray for the pastors and leaders of your church. Use the space provided to write down their names and specific petitions you can offer up to God on their behalf.

_____

_____

_____

_____

_____

_____

_____

_____

_____

THE BELOVED BROTHER TYCHICUS

So they'd know how to pray specifically for him, Paul sent Tychicus to deliver this letter and the letter to the church in Colossae. Tychicus was a believer from Asia who was with Paul during this first Roman imprisonment and was very helpful to him, as is evidenced by Paul sending him on several missions (2 Timothy 4:12;

Titus 3:12). He was a beloved brother and faithful friend in ministry, and Paul knew that his report would encourage and comfort the Ephesian believers.

Read Ephesians 6:23–24. How does Paul end this letter?

_____

_____

_____

Paul ends this letter by bringing together the main themes of his writing: peace brought about because of the incredible love of God, love for all the saints, and faith because they'd been made one in Christ through faith in Him.

e. (embrace)

In a few sentences, summarize the book of Ephesians. What has impacted you most through this study?

_____

_____

_____

_____

_____

_____

IN SUMMARY . . .

Ephesians teaches that we're all dead in our trespasses and sins. On the inside our hearts are tainted with selfishness, pride, and a desire to control our own lives. We're ruled by the power of this world and headed for an eternity in hell, separated from the God who created us. But God, who is rich in mercy because of His great love for us, sent His one and only Son to redeem us through His blood, making us alive in Him.

Before the foundation of the world, you and I were chosen by God and predestined to be His sons and daughters. When we say yes to following Jesus—when we die to self, repent, confess, and actively believe in Christ's redemptive work on the cross—our lives are transformed and we're led from the shallows into deep faith in Jesus. Our once sin-tainted lives are covered by the precious blood of Jesus, and He bridges the gap between us and God. The Holy Spirit makes known to us our mission here on earth, equipping us with spiritual gifts so our deep faith in Jesus can seep into our outside living. This enables us to help others find deep faith, beyond the shallow religion that leaves them settling for less than what God intends for their lives.

The mission is laced with struggle and battle, though. The enemy is still on the prowl, seeking whom he may devour and desperately trying to render all Christians ineffective for God's kingdom. But again, our merciful, loving God has provided for us protection and power against the enemy. He has given us His spiritual armor as our defense in the battle we fight against Satan and his demons.

We have no need to fear. No need to cower. No need to live defeated. For we are more than conquerors in Christ (Romans 8:37)!

A Final Word

Oh, dear friend, you did it! You just went through a whole book of the New Testament, diving deeper into God's Word. I'm so proud of you! I know the choice to d.i.v.e. deeper wasn't an easy one to make; there's so much vying for our time and attention. I pray this is only the first of many d.i.v.e.s you'll make into God's Word. He has so much to teach us all. Use the tools you've been given and continue to make the one choice that will radically change your life, leading you to find deep faith beyond shallow religion.

As we end our time together in Ephesians, I want to encourage you with the same promises I shared with you at the beginning of our time together. I have no doubt that as you continue to study God's Word, three great things will result:

- God will meet you on the pages of Scripture and teach you Himself.

- The Holy Spirit will open your eyes, heart, and mind, giving you the wisdom to know how to apply God's Word to your life.

- And one more thing . . . God will transform your life as you study His Word and come to know Him more, I promise He will!

I am before the throne for you! Continue to make the choice to d.i.v.e. deeper! You've been transformed, mighty warrior girl, from the inside out! Live out and walk worthy of the calling to which you've been called, and continue to d.i.v.e. deeper into the Source, stepping forward from the shallows into deep faith in Jesus!

Keep diving deeper,

Bible Study Tools

Tools to Help You d.i.v.e. deeper into the Word

 Scuba divers must have the proper gear to dive into the deepest depths of the ocean. The same is true for students of the Word; they must have the right gear and tools to d.i.v.e deeper into God's Word.

Here are a handful of tools available to help you d.i.v.e. deeper into God's Word.

Commentaries (1 volume)

- *A Survey of the New Testament* by Robert H. Gundry
- *Matthew Henry's Concise Commentary on the Whole Bible* by Matthew Henry
- *Old Testament Teaching* by J. Wash Watts
- *Talk thru the Bible* by Bruce Wilkinson and Kenneth Boa

Commentaries (multivolume)

- *The MacArthur New Testament Commentary* (29 volumes) by John MacArthur (purchase separately as you study different books of the Bible)
- *The Bible Knowledge Commentary*, Old and New Testaments (2 volumes), edited by John F. Walvoord and Roy B. Zuck

- *The Expositor's Bible Commentary* (12 volumes), edited by Frank E. Gaebelein (Zondervan)

- *The New American Commentary* (multiple volumes, Old Testament and New Testament), Broadman and Holman Publishing Group

- *The Wiersbe Bible Commentary*, Old and New Testaments (2 volumes), by Warren W. Wiersbe

- *Women's Evangelical Commentary*, Old and New Testaments (2 volumes), by Dorothy Kelley Patterson and Rhonda Harrington Kelley

- *Zondervan NIV Bible Commentary*, Old and New Testaments (2 volumes), by Kenneth L. Barker and III John R. Kohlenberger

Dictionaries and Concordances

- *Dictionary of Jesus and the Gospels*, edited by Joel B. Green, Scot McKnight, and I. Howard Marshall

- *Dictionary of New Testament Background* by Craig A. Evans and Stanley E. Porter

- *The IVP Bible Dictionary* series, various editors

- *Evangelical Dictionary of Theology* (Baker Reference Library) by Walter A. Elwell

- *Holman Illustrated Bible Dictionary* by Charles W. Draper, Chad Brand and Archie England

- *Strong's Exhaustive Concordance of the Bible* (KJV) by James Strong

- *Thayer's Greek-English Lexicon of the New Testament* by Joseph Thayer

- *The Complete Word Study: Old Testament* by Spiros Zodhiates and Dr. Warren Patrick Baker; and *The Complete Word Study: New Testament* by Spiros Zodhiates
- *Vine's Complete Expository Dictionary of Old and New Testament Words* by W. E. Vine

Study Bibles

- ESV Study Bible
- Hebrew-Greek Key Word Study Bible
- The MacArthur Study Bible
- Life Application Study Bible

Books about the Bible

- *Explore the Book: A Survey and Study of Each Book from Genesis Through Revelation*, by J. Sidlow Baxter
- *How to Read the Bible for All Its Worth* by Gordon D. Fee and Douglas Stuart
- *How to Read the Bible Book by Book: A Guided Tour* by Gordon D. Fee and Douglas Stuart
- *The Eerdman's Companion to the Bible* by Gordon D. Fee and Robert L. Hubbard Jr.

Theology Books

- *Christian Theology* by Millard J. Erickson
- *Systematic Theology* by Wayne Grudem

Online Tools (free)

- Bible Gateway, http://biblegateway.com *(I especially enjoy this for its wide assortment of translations.)*
- Bible Map, http://www.biblemap.org
- Bible Study Tools, http://www.biblestudytools.com

Software

- e-Sword, http://www.e-sword.net *(Several of the tools used in this book are available on this site free or for a minimal charge.)*
- Logos Bible Software, http://www.logos.com
- WORDsearch, http://www.wordsearchbible.com
- BibleWorks, http://www.bibleworks.com

A Simple Guide to Finding the Right Bible for You

Choosing the Right Bible Translation

The Bible was originally written in Hebrew, Aramaic, and Greek. Over many years, scholars have translated the original text into numerous translations, which generally fall into four categories:

Formal equivalence, **also known as a literal or word-for-word translation,** seeks to retain the form of the Hebrew or Greek while producing basically understandable English. Formal equivalence also seeks to reproduce the grammar or syntax (pattern) of the original text as closely as possible.[1] A few versions that fall into this category:

- King James Version (KJV)
- New King James Version (NKJV)
- New American Standard Bible (NASB)
- English Standard Version (ESV)
- Amplified (AMP)

Functional equivalence **(originally called dynamic equivalence), also known as thought-for-thought or meaning-based,** seeks to reproduce its meaning in good idiomatic (natural) English. These words are translated according to their meaning in context rather than according to lexical concordance.[2] A few versions that fall into this category:

- Living Bible (TLB)
- Contemporary English Version (CEV)
- New Living Translation (NLT)
- New Century Version (NCV)
- The Message (MSG)

Mediating, **also known as word-for-word and thought-for-thought** combined. This translation represents a middle ground between formal equivalence and functional equivalence, seeking to maintain a balance between form and function.[3] A few versions that fall into this category:

- Holman Christian Standard Bible (HSCB)
- New International Version (NIV)
- New English Translation (NET)

Contextual equivalence seeks to convey the original language accurately while rendering the literary structures and character of a text in a readable and meaningful contemporary language. Recognizing that context is the most important factor in determining the meaning of a word, sentence, paragraph, or narrative, this translation seeks to preserve both the linguistic and literary features of the original biblical text.[4] A version that falls into this category:

- *The Voice*

Getting to Know Your Bible

The *table of contents* is a list of the books of the Bible, page numbers, and other information contained within the Bible.

Book introductions give a brief overview of each book of the Bible. Here you'll find a brief explanation of the book's title, the author, the date the book was written, the background and setting, themes, and an outline.

Chapter divisions break down the chapter into a more readable form.

Cross-references identify similar passages of Scripture and are usually found in the center or side margins.

Translation notes give the original meaning of the wordage that has been used.

Study notes provide a deeper look into specific verses.

A *topical index*, usually found in the back of a Bible, gives references to specific topics.

Investigative Questions That Lead to Important Spiritual Discoveries

Asking WHO . . .

WHO wrote this?

To WHOM was it written?

WHO are the characters involved?

Asking WHAT . . .

WHAT is the author talking about?

WHAT is going on?

WHAT does this word mean?

Asking WHEN . . .

WHEN did this event happen (past)?

WHEN will this event happen (future)?

Asking WHERE . . .

WHERE did this happen?

WHERE did the characters go?

WHERE are they going next?

Asking WHY . . .

WHY did this happen?

WHY was that said?

WHY did the characters go where they went?

WHY is this important to me?

Asking HOW . . .

HOW did that happen?

HOW did the people know it had happened?

HOW can I apply this to my life?

Implant. Embrace. Enact.

 Scripture memorization is essential in the life of every believer. Here are five reasons why we must commit to implanting God's Word deep within our heart . . .

ONE: to become more like Christ

Implanting God's Word in our hearts, fixing our gaze upon Him through the Scriptures, reveals to us His true nature and character. This revelation ushers us into the reality of knowing Him more and reflecting His person. Paul wrote that "we are being transformed, *metamorphosed*, into His same image from one radiance of glory to another, just as the Spirit of the Lord accomplishes it" (2 Corinthians 3:18).

TWO: to experience victory over sin

"How can a young person remain pure? *Only* by living according to Your word. . . . Deep within me I have hidden Your word so that I will never sin against You" (Psalm 119:9, 11). The one piece of the armor of God that is used to kill is the "sword of the Spirit," (Ephesians 6:17) the Word of God. Daily we're confronted with the choice to sin or to walk according to God's way. When this choice arises, we can call to mind God's Word and experience victory over the temptation to choose sin over God's way.

THREE: to daily defeat the enemy, Satan

When Jesus was tempted by Satan in the wilderness, He recited Scripture from memory to stand again Satan (Matthew 4:1–11).

FOUR: to encourage those in need

When our friends and families need an encouraging word, we may not always have our Bibles handy. But with God's Word implanted in our hearts, those words are able to freely flow anytime and anywhere. Not only that, when the Word of God is spoken, it has unusual power. Proverbs 25:11 says, "A well-spoken word *at just the right moment* is like golden apples in settings of silver."

FIVE: to share the Gospel with unbelievers

Opportunities to share the Good News with those who don't have a relationship with God often come about when we don't have a Bible close by. We must learn God's Word and implant it deep within our hearts so we're able to share God's message of redemption when He brings an unbeliever into our lives.

HOW TO MEMORIZE GOD'S WORD

Now that we know the why behind implanting God's Word in our hearts, let's discover the how. When it comes to memorizing God's Word, one size doesn't fit all—there are numerous ways to ingest and digest the Scriptures. The method or plan used to devour the Word is yours for the choosing. Some prefer a very structured approach to memorizing Scriptures, others are creative in their memorization, and still others prefer to set their verses to music. Do what works for you!

Whatever method is used to implant the Word, here are a few things to keep in mind:

1. *Implant it.* Implant the verse deep within your heart by repeating it numerous times a day.

2. *Read the verse in context.* Reading the verse in context is important because it will help you better understand the meaning of the verse, memorize the verse, and use the verse in the right manner (2 Timothy 2:15).

3. *Learn the location of the verse.* Say the reference at the beginning of the verse. Say the verse. Say the reference at the end of the verse.

4. *Break the verse down into small bites.* How do you eat an elephant? One bite at a time! You memorize a verse of Scripture one phrase at a time. Look for key words in each phrase. Say the reference and then the phrase. Repeat these steps and add the next phrase until you have memorized the entire verse.

5. *Write down the verse and look at it.* Get a visual image of the verse. Highlight or underline key words in the verse that can help you link phrases. Record the verse on a card. Write the verse on one side of the card and the reference on the opposite side.

6. *Learn the verse word perfectly.* Be precise in your memorization. Take note of the punctuation marks. Don't overlook even the smallest words—they often make the biggest difference. Learning a verse perfectly will give you confidence in using the verse.

7. *Embrace it.* Embrace the verse you've just implanted by continuing to cling to it along with each new verse you memorize.

8. *Review it.* Memorization is only half the battle. You must review your verses every day.

- Keep a memory card with you at all times.
- Make a prayer from the verse.
- Apply the verse to your life.
- Review your verses with a family member or friend.

9. *Enact it.* Enact the verses you've implanted by putting them into action. Don't just memorize the Word; live it!

A few other ideas for implanting the Word:

1. Doodle, draw, or use other types of creative art to express yourself as you memorize the Scriptures.

2. Pray the Word. Take the verses you're learning and pray them back to God; doing this will make those verses become part of who you are.

3. Set the verses you are memorizing to the tune of your favorite song.

Notes

SECTION 1: IN HIM

Lesson 1: An Unlikely Becomes Extraordinary

1. Thayer's Greek Definitions, e-Sword Bible software (Rick Meyers). http://www.e-sword.net/index.html.
2. Trent C. Butler, gen. ed., *Holman Bible Dictionary* (Nashville: Holman Bible Publishers, 1991), 573.
3. Thayer's Greek Definitions.
4. Butler, 1086.

Lesson 2: "Let Me In!"

1. Bible Study Tools, "tselem"; accessed September 16, 2013, http://www .biblestudytools.com/lexicons/hebrew/kjv/tselem.html.
2. StudyLight.org, "tselem" (Strong's 6754); accessed September 16, 2013, http://www.studylight.org/ls/ht/index.cgi?a=592.
3. Thayer's Greek Definitions, e-Sword Bible software (Rick Meyers). http://www.e-sword.net/index.html.
4. Klyne Snodgrass, *The NIV Application Commentary: Ephesians* (Grand Rapids: Zondervan, 1996), 51.
5. Thayer's Greek Definitions.
6. Ibid.
7. John Piper, "Sealed by the Spirit to the Day of Redemption" (sermon transcript), May 6, 1984, Desiring God, http://www.desiringgod.org/ resource-library/sermons/sealed-by-the-spirit-to-the-day-of-redemption.

Lesson 3: Meaning Behind the Message

1. Thayer's Greek Definitions, e-Sword Bible software (Rick Meyers). http://www.e-sword.net/index.html
2. Warren W. Wiersbe, *The Wiersbe Bible Commentary, NT* (Colorado Springs: David C. Cook, 2007), 590.

SECTION 2: OPERATION PEACE

Lesson 3: He Is Our Peace

1. Trent C. Butler, gen. ed., *Holman Bible Dictionary* (Nashville: Holman Bible Publishers, 1991), 1086.

2. John MacArthur, *The MacArthur New Testament Commentary: Ephesians* (Chicago: Moody, 1986), 77.

3. Thayer's Greek Definitions, e-Sword Bible software (Rick Meyers). http://www.e-sword.net/index.html.

SECTION 3: HE'S GOT THE WHOLE WORLD IN HIS HANDS . . . THAT INCLUDES YOU

Lesson 1: God's Mystery Made Known

1. Thayer's Greek Definitions, e-Sword Bible software (Rick Meyers). http://www.e-sword.net/index.html.

2. John MacArthur, *The MacArthur New Testament Commentary: Ephesians* (Chicago: Moody, 1986), 98.

3. Rick Warren, *The Purpose Driven Life: What On Earth Am I Here For?* (2002; repr., Grand Rapids: Zondervan, 2012), 314–15.

Lesson 2: Worship the Lord

1. Frank Whaling, ed., *John and Charles Wesley: Selected Writings and Hymns* (New York: Paulist Press, 1981), 387.

2. John MacArthur, *The MacArthur New Testament Commentary: Ephesians* (Chicago: Moody, 1986), 104; bold and italics in original.

3. Thayer's Greek Definitions, e-Sword Bible software (Rick Meyers). http://www.e-sword.net/index.html.

4. John Barnett, *Revelation from Now to Forever* (n.p.: BFM Books, 2004), 732.

SECTION 4: SO HAPPY TOGETHER

Lesson 1: From Knowledge to Action

1. John MacArthur, *The MacArthur New Testament Commentary: Ephesians* (Chicago: Moody, 1986), 124–25.

2. Spiros Zodhiates, *The Complete Word Study New Testament* (Chattanooga, TN: AMG, 1991), 934.

3. MacArthur, 128.

Lesson 2: Off with the Old, on with the New

1. Strong's Hebrew and Greek Dictionaries, e-Sword Bible software (Rick Meyers). http://www.e-sword.net/index.html.pōrōsis- stupidity or callousness

Lesson 3: Standards for New Living

1. John MacArthur, *The MacArthur New Testament Commentary: Ephesians* (Chicago: Moody, 1986), 196.

 # SECTION 5: MONKEY SEE, MONKEY DO

Lesson 1: Have NO Part In . . .

1. Thayer's Greek Definitions, e-Sword Bible software (Rick Meyers). http://www.e-sword.net/index.html.
2. "Statistics," Transforming Hope Ministries website, accessed September 19, 2013, http://www.transforminghopeministries.org/#!get-educated/c21kz.
3. "What is Human Trafficking," University at Albany website, accessed October 11, 2013, http://ualbanyhtconference2013.weebly.com/what-is-human-trafficking.html.

Lesson 3: Strength in Submission

1. Thayer's Greek Definitions, e-Sword Bible software (Rick Meyers). http://www.e-sword.net/index.html.
2. Ibid.
3. John Gill, *John Gill's Exposition of the Entire Bible*, e-Sword Bible software (Rick Meyers). http://www.e-sword.net/index.html.
4. Bob Deffinbaugh, "Taking a Second Look at Submission (1 Peter 2:13–3:7)," from the series *The Glory of Suffering—Studies in 1 Peter*, July 3, 2004, Bible.org, https://bible.org/seriespage/taking-second-look-submission-1-peter-213-37.

 # SECTION 6: WARRIOR GIRL

Lesson 1: The Believer's Role

1. James Strong, *Strong's Hebrew and Greek Dictionaries*, e-Sword Bible software (Rick Meyers). http://www.e-sword.net/index.html.
2. Ibid.

Lesson 2: Where's the Love?

1. John MacArthur, *The MacArthur New Testament Commentary: Ephesians* (Chicago: Moody, 1986), 331.
2. James Strong, *Strong's Hebrew and Greek Dictionaries*, e-Sword Bible software (Rick Meyers). http://www.e-sword.net/index.html.
3. MacArthur, 368.

Lesson 3: Pray Without Ceasing

1. John MacArthur, *The MacArthur New Testament Commentary: Ephesians* (Chicago: Moody, 1986), 377.

 # APPENDIX II

1. Gordon D. Fee and Mark L. Strauss, *How to Choose a Translation for All Its Worth: A Guide to Understanding and Using Bible Versions* (Grand Rapids: Zondervan, 2007), 26.
2. Ibid., 26–27.
3. Ibid., 28.
4. *The Voice* (Nashville: Thomas Nelson, 2012), 19.

Acknowledgments

We've been to the
depths together.
You've blessed me much.
With all my heart I thank you.
Now . . . let's keep diving
deeper with Jesus!

JGBS • HFBC Ladies Bible Study • Internet Café
Devotions • Thomas Nelson Team • Harper Collins
Christian Publishing Team • Sarah • Heather • Ashley •
Donna • Wendy • Amanda • Alee • Jennifer • Bethany
• Blythe • Frank • Jerri • Kim • Marilyn • Debra • Tracy •
Lorri • Laura • Lisa •Pam G. • Kelli • Wrenne • Jessica
• Sonya • Pam • Heidi • Sandy • Lisa B. • Yancy • Tina
• Sarah D. • Patti • Robin • Ms. Trudy • Carolyn • Lori •
Linda • Elisa • Sue • Carol • Alisa • Ms. Margaret • Jill •
Mack • Jesse • Leah • Josh • Mom • Dad •
Lydia • Will • Hannah • Chris

Diving Deeper Ministries exists for the purpose of leading and equipping women of all ages to d.i.v.e. deeper into God's Word and live abundantly in Christ.

Through the expository teaching of God's Word in local and online Bible studies, devotional writings, women's conferences and retreats, women of all ages are led to understand the magnitude of God's abundant grace and the freedom that grace brings into their lives. They're taught to d.i.v.e. deeper into God's Word for themselves, developing an intimate relationship with their Savior while discovering their God given gifts. Women are then encouraged to go back into their local churches and communities, utilizing their gifts to grow and benefit the body of Christ.

Join Jenifer for *a Diving Deeper Experience* where you'll learn to back-stroke through the pages of God's Word. *A Diving Deeper Experience* is an **interactive experience** that answers the hows, whys, and whats of diving deeper into God's life-changing Word; an experience that will equip you with practical tools for lifelong study of the Scriptures.

Be challenged to

- dive deeper into intimate relationship with Jesus Christ,
- dive deeper into abundant living,
- and dive deeper into purposed action.

Find out more about Jenifer and Diving Deeper Ministries at jeniferjernigan.com. And while you're there, be sure to check out free companion resources for Dive Deeper: Finding Deep Faith Beyond Shallow Religion.

READ MORE FROM THE INSCRIBED COLLECTION

— AVAILABLE NOW —

— COMING FALL 2014 —

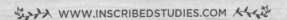

SHARE THE INSCRIBED COLLECTION

EXPERIENCE THE BOOKS

Your friends can sample this book or any of our InScribed titles for FREE. Visit InScribedStudies.com and select any of our titles to learn how.

Know a church, ministry, or small group that would benefit from these readings? Contact your favorite bookseller or visit InScribedStudies.com/ buy-in-bulk for bulk purchasing information.

CONNECT WITH THE AUTHORS

Do you want to get to know more about the author of this book or any of the authors in the InScribed Collection? Go online to InScribedStudies.com to see how you could meet them through a Google Hangout or connect with them through our InScribed Facebook.

JOIN IN THE CONVERSATION

 Like facebook.com/InScribedStudies and be the first to see new videos, discounts, and updates from the InScribed Studies team.

 Start following @InScribedStudy.

 Follow our author's boards @InScribedStudies.

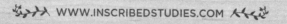 WWW.INSCRIBEDSTUDIES.COM